Wild at Heart

This Large Print Book carries the
Seal of Approval of N.A.V.H.

Wild at Heart

Discovering the Secret of a Man's Soul

JOHN ELDREDGE

Walker Large Print • Waterville, Maine

Published in 2004 by arrangement with Thomas Nelson, Inc.

The text of this Large Print edition is unabridged.
Other aspects of the book may vary from the original edition.

Set in 16 pt. Plantin by Al Chase.

Printed in the United States on permanent paper.

Library of Congress Cataloging-in-Publication Data

Eldredge, John.
    Wild at heart : discovering the secret of a man's soul /
John Eldredge.
        p. cm.
    Includes bibliographical references.
    ISBN 1-59415-016-8 (lg. print : sc : alk. paper)
    1. Christian men — Religious life. 2. Masculinity —
Religious aspects — Christianity. 3. Large type books.
I. Title.
BV4528.2E45 2004
248.8'42—dc22   2003057587

For Samuel, Blaine, and Luke.

I love your warrior hearts. You definitely have what it takes.

As the Founder/CEO of NAVH, the only national health agency solely devoted to those who, although not totally blind, have an eye disease which could lead to serious visual impairment, I am pleased to recognize Thorndike Press* as one of the leading publishers in the large print field.

Founded in 1954 in San Francisco to prepare large print textbooks for partially seeing children, NAVH became the pioneer and standard setting agency in the preparation of large type.

Today, those publishers who meet our standards carry the prestigious "Seal of Approval" indicating high quality large print. We are delighted that Thorndike Press is one of the publishers whose titles meet these standards. We are also pleased to recognize the significant contribution Thorndike Press is making in this important and growing field.

Lorraine H. Marchi, L.H.D.
Founder/CEO
NAVH

* Thorndike Press encompasses the following imprints: Thorndike, Wheeler, Walker and Large Print Press.

I have just finished reading John Eldredge's new work, *Wild at Heart*. I was deeply moved by this excellent book. I believe it is the best, most insightful book I have read in at least the last five years. I plan to read it again through the summer, only this next time, much more slowly. Eldredge shares splendid ideas that he has stated so creatively and, thankfully, free of cliché. New vistas will appear in the readers' minds as they take the wonderful journey of reading this book. His insights on identifying the wound, facing it head-on, then staying with it until the healing transpires will be immensely helpful to many folks. Every man and his wife and every mother of a boy really should read this book.

CHARLES R. SWINDOLL
June 28, 2001

Acknowledgments

My deep thanks to those who have helped me climb this mountain:

Sam, Blaine, Jenny, Aaron, Morgan, Cherie, Julie, Gary, Leigh, Travis, Sealy, and Stasi. Brian and Kyle at Thomas Nelson. The Thursday night poker group. And all those who have been praying for me, near and far.

Brent, for teaching me more about what it means to be a man than anyone else ever has, and Craig, for taking up the sword.

Contents

Introduction

I know. I almost want to apologize. *Dear Lord — do we really need another book for men?*

Nope. We need something else. We need *permission*.

Permission to be what we are — men made in God's image. Permission to live from the heart and not from the list of "should" and "ought to" that has left so many of us tired and bored.

Most messages for men ultimately fail. The reason is simple: They ignore what is deep and true to a man's *heart,* his real passions, and simply try to shape him up through various forms of pressure. "This is the man you *ought* to be. This is what a good husband/father/Christian/churchgoer *ought* to do." Fill in the blanks from there. He is responsible, sensitive, disciplined, faithful, diligent, dutiful, etc. Many of these are good qualities. That these messengers are well-intentioned I have no doubt. But the road to hell, as we remember, is paved with good intentions. That they are a near total failure should seem obvious by now.

No, men need something else. They need a deeper understanding of why they long for adventures and battles and a Beauty — and why God made them *just like that.* And they need a deeper understanding of why women long to be fought for, to be swept up into adventure, and to *be* the Beauty. For that is how God made them as well.

So I offer this book, not as the seven steps to being a better Christian, but as a safari of the heart to recover a life of freedom, passion, and adventure. I believe it will help men get their heart back — and women as well. Moreover, it will help women to understand their men and help them live the life they both want. That is my prayer for you.

It is not the critic who counts, not the man who points out how the strong man stumbles, or where the doer of deeds could have done them better. The credit belongs to the man in the arena, whose face is marred by dust and sweat and blood, who strives valiantly . . . who knows the great enthusiasms, the great devotions, who spends himself in a worthy cause, who at the best knows in the end the triumph of high achievement, and who at the worst, if he fails, at least fails while daring greatly, so that his place shall never be with those cold and timid souls who have never known neither victory nor defeat.

— TEDDY ROOSEVELT

The kingdom of heaven suffers violence, and violent men take it by force.

— MATTHEW 11:12 NASB

Chapter One

WILD AT HEART

The heart of a man is like deep water . . .
                                    — PROVERBS 20:5 NKJV

The spiritual life cannot be made suburban. It is always frontier, and we who live in it must accept and even rejoice that it remains untamed.
                                    — HOWARD MACEY

*I want to ride to the ridge where the west
        commences
I can't look at hobbles and I can't stand fences
Don't fence me in.*
                                    — COLE PORTER
                                    "Don't Fence Me In"

At last, I am surrounded by wilderness. The wind in the top of the pines behind me sounds like the ocean. Waves are rushing in from the great blue above, cresting upon the ridge of the mountain I have climbed, somewhere in the Sawatch Range of central Colorado. Spreading out below me the landscape is a sea of sagebrush for mile after lonesome mile. Zane Grey immortalized it as the purple sage, but most of the year it's more of a silver gray. This is the kind of country you could ride across for days on horseback without seeing another living soul. Today, I am on foot. Though the sun is shining this afternoon, it will not warm above thirty here near the Continental Divide, and the sweat I worked up scaling this face is now making me shiver. It is late October and winter is coming on. In the distance, nearly a hundred miles south by southwest, the San Juan Mountains are already covered in snow.

The aroma of the pungent sage still clings to my jeans, and it clears my head as I gasp for air — in notably short supply at 10,000 feet. I am forced to rest again, even though I know that each pause broadens the distance between me and my quarry. Still, the advantage has always been his. Though the tracks I found this morning were fresh — only a few hours old — that holds little promise. A bull elk can easily cover miles of rugged country in that amount of time, especially if he is wounded or on the run.

The wapiti, as the Indians called him, is one of the most elusive creatures we have left in the lower forty-eight. They are the ghost kings of the high country, more cautious and wary than deer, and more difficult to track. They live at higher elevations, and travel farther in a day, than nearly any other game. The bulls especially seem to carry a sixth sense to human presence. A few times I've gotten close; the next moment they are gone, vanishing silently into aspen groves so thick you wouldn't have believed a rabbit could get through.

It wasn't always this way. For centuries elk lived out on the prairies, grazing together on the rich grasses in vast numbers. In the spring of 1805 Meriwether Lewis described passing herds lolling about in the thousands as he made his way in search of a Northwest Passage. At times the curious wandered so close he could throw sticks at them, like bucolic dairy cows blocking the road. But by the end of the century westward expansion had pushed the elk high up into the Rocky Mountains. Now they are elusive, hiding out at timberline like outlaws until heavy snows force them down for the winter. If you would seek them now, it is on their terms, in forbidding haunts well beyond the reach of civilization.

And that is why I come.

And why I linger here still, letting the old bull get away. My hunt, you see, actually has little to do with elk. I knew that before I came. There is something else I am after, out here in the wild. I am searching for an even more elusive prey . . . something that can only be found through the help of wilderness.

I am looking for my heart.

WILD AT HEART

Eve was created within the lush beauty of Eden's garden. But Adam, if you'll remember, was created *outside* the Garden, in the wilderness. In the record of our beginnings, the second chapter of Genesis makes it clear: Man was born in the outback, from the untamed part of creation. Only afterward is he brought to Eden. And ever since then boys have never been at home indoors, and men have had an insatiable longing to explore. We long to return; it's when most men come alive. As John Muir said, when a man comes to the mountains, he comes home. The core of a man's heart is undomesticated *and that is*

18

good. "I am not alive in an office," as one Northface ad has it. "I am not alive in a taxi cab. I am not alive on a sidewalk." Amen to that. Their conclusion? "Never stop exploring."

My gender seems to need little encouragement. It comes naturally, like our innate love of maps. In 1260 Marco Polo headed off to find China, and in 1967, when I was seven, I tried to dig a hole straight through from our backyard with my friend Danny Wilson. We gave up at about eight feet, but it made a great fort. Hannibal crosses his famous Alps, and there comes a day in a boy's life when he first crosses the street and enters the company of the great explorers. Scott and Amundsen race for the South Pole, Peary and Cook vie for the North, and when last summer I gave my boys some loose change and permission to ride their bikes down to the store to buy a soda, you'd have thought I'd given them a charter to go find the equator. Magellan sails due west, around the tip of South America — despite warnings that he and his crew will drop off the end of the earth — and Huck Finn heads off down the Mississippi ignoring similar threats. Powell follows the Colorado into the Grand Canyon, even though — no, *because* — no one has done it before and

19

everyone is saying it can't be done.

And so my boys and I stood on the bank of the Snake River in the spring of '98, feeling that ancient urge to shove off. Snow melt was high that year, unusually high, and the river had overflowed its banks and was surging through the trees on both sides. Out in the middle of the river, which is crystal clear in late summer but that day looked like chocolate milk, logs were floating down, large tangles of branches bigger than a car, and who knows what else. High and muddy and fast, the Snake was forbidding. No other rafters could be seen. Did I mention it was raining? But we had a brand-new canoe and the paddles were in hand and, sure, I have never floated the Snake in a canoe, nor any other river for that matter, but what the heck. We jumped in and headed off into the unknown, like Livingstone plunging into the interior of dark Africa.

Adventure, with all its requisite danger and wildness, is a deeply spiritual longing written into the soul of man. The masculine heart needs a place where nothing is prefabricated, modular, nonfat, zip lock, franchised, on-line, microwavable. Where there are no deadlines, cell phones, or committee meetings. Where there is room for the soul. Where, finally, the geography around us corresponds to the geography of our heart. Look at the heroes of the biblical text: Moses does not encounter the living God at the mall. He finds him (or is found by him) somewhere out in the deserts of Sinai, a long way from the comforts of Egypt. The same is true of Jacob, who has his wrestling match with God not on the living room sofa but in a wadi somewhere east of the Jabbok, in Mesopotamia. Where did the great prophet Elijah go to recover his strength? To the wild. As did John the Baptist, and his cousin, Jesus, who is *led by the Spirit* into the wilderness.

Whatever else those explorers were after, they were also searching for themselves. Deep in a man's heart are some fundamental questions that simply cannot be answered at the kitchen table. Who am I? What am I made of? What am I destined for? It is fear that keeps a man at home where things are neat and orderly *and under his control.* But the answers to his deepest questions are not to be found on television or in the refrigerator. Out there on the burning desert sands, lost in a trackless waste, Moses received his life's mission and purpose. He is called out, called up into something much bigger than he ever imagined, much more serious than CEO or "prince of Egypt." Under foreign stars, in the dead of night, Jacob received a new name, his real name. No longer is he a shrewd business negotiator, but now he is one who wrestles with God. The wilderness trial of Christ is, at its core, a test of his *identity*. "If you are who you think you are . . ." If a man is ever to find out who he is and what he's here for, he has got to take that journey for himself.

He has got to get his heart back.

WESTWARD EXPANSION AGAINST THE SOUL

The way a man's life unfolds nowadays tends to drive his heart into remote regions of the soul. Endless hours at a computer screen; selling shoes at the mall; meetings, memos, phone calls. The business world — where the majority of American men live and die — requires a man to be efficient and punctual. Corporate policies and procedures are designed with one aim: to harness a man to the plow and make him produce. But the soul refuses to be harnessed; it knows nothing of Day Timers and deadlines and P&L statements. The soul longs for passion, for freedom, for *life*. As D. H. Lawrence said, "I am not a mechanism." A man needs to feel the rhythms of the earth; he needs to have in hand something real — the tiller of a boat, a set of reins, the roughness of rope, or simply a shovel. Can a man live all his days to keep his fingernails clean and trim? Is that what a boy dreams of?

Society at large can't make up its mind about men. Having spent the last thirty years redefining masculinity into something more sensitive, safe, manageable and, well, feminine, it now berates men for not being men. Boys will be boys, they sigh. As though if a man were to truly grow up he would forsake wilderness and wanderlust and settle down, be at home forever in Aunt Polly's parlor. "Where are all the *real* men?" is regular fare for talk shows and new books. *You asked them to be women,* I want to say. The result is a gender confusion never experienced at such a wide level in the history of the world. How can a man know he is one when his highest aim is minding his manners?

And then, alas, there is the church. Christianity, as it currently exists, has done some terrible things to men. When all is said and done, I think most men in the church believe that God put them on the earth to be a good boy. The problem with men, we are told, is that they don't know how to keep their promises, be spiritual leaders, talk to their wives, or raise their children. But, if they will try real hard they can reach the lofty summit of becoming . . . a nice guy. That's what we hold up as models of Christian maturity: Really Nice Guys. We don't smoke, drink, or swear; that's what makes us *men*. Now let me ask my male readers: In all your boyhood dreams growing up, did you ever dream of becoming a Nice Guy? (Ladies, was the Prince of your dreams dashing . . . or merely nice?)

Really now — do I overstate my case? Walk into most churches in America, have a look around, and ask yourself this question: What is a Christian man? Don't listen to what is said, look at what you find there. There is no doubt about it. You'd have to admit a Christian man is . . . bored. At a recent church retreat I was talking with a guy in his fifties, listening really, about his own journey as a man. "I've pretty much tried for the last twenty years to be a good man as the church defines it." Intrigued, I asked him to say what he thought that was. He paused for a long moment. "Dutiful," he said. "And separated from his heart." *A perfect description*, I thought. *Sadly right on the mark.*

As Robert Bly laments in *Iron John*,

"Some women want a passive man if they want a man at all, the church wants a tamed man — they are called priests, the university wants a domesticated man — they are called tenure-track people, the corporation wants a . . . sanitized, hairless, shallow man." It all comes together as a sort of westward expansion against the masculine soul. And thus the *heart* of a man is driven into the high country, into remote places, like a wounded animal looking for cover. Women know this, and lament that they have no access to their man's heart. Men know it, too, but are often unable to explain why their heart is missing. They know their heart is on the run, but they often do not know where to pick up the trail. The church wags its head and wonders why it can't get more men to sign up for its programs. The answer is simply this: We have not invited a man to know and live from his deep heart.

AN INVITATION

But God made the masculine heart, set it within every man, and thereby offers him an *invitation:* Come, and live out what I meant you to be. Permit me to bypass the entire nature vs. nurture "is gender really built-in?" debate with one simple observation: Men and women are made in the image of God *as men* or *as women*. "So God created man in his own image, in the image of God he created him, male and female he created them" (Gen. 1:27). Now, we know God doesn't have a body, so the uniqueness can't be physical. Gender simply must be at the level of the soul, in the deep and everlasting places within us. God doesn't make generic people; he makes something very distinct — a man or a woman. In other words, there is a masculine heart and a feminine heart, which in their own ways reflect or portray to the world God's heart.

God *meant* something when he meant man, and if we are to ever find ourselves we must find that. What has he set in the masculine heart? Instead of asking what you think you ought to do to become a better man (or woman, for my female readers), I want to ask, *What makes you come alive?* What stirs your heart? The journey we face now is into a land foreign to most of us. We must head into country that has no clear trail. This charter for exploration takes us into our own hearts, into our deepest desires. As the playwright Christopher Fry says,

Life is a hypocrite if I can't live
The way it moves me!

There are three desires I find written so deeply into my heart I know now I can no longer disregard them without losing my soul. They are core to who and what I am and yearn to be. I gaze into boyhood, I search the pages of literature, I listen carefully to many, many men, and I am convinced these desires are universal, a clue into masculinity itself. They may be misplaced, forgotten, or misdirected, but in the heart of every man is a desperate desire for a battle to fight, an adventure to live, and a beauty to rescue. I want you to think of the films men love, the things they do with their free time, and especially the aspirations of little boys and see if I am not right on this.

A BATTLE TO FIGHT

There's a photo on my wall of a little boy about five years old, with a crew cut, big cheeks, and an impish grin. It's an old photograph, and the color is fading, but the image is timeless. It's Christmas morning, 1964, and I've just opened what may have been the best present any boy received on any Christmas ever — a set of two pearl-handled six-shooters, complete with black leather holsters, a red cowboy shirt with two wild mustangs embroidered on either breast, shiny black boots, red bandanna, and straw hat. I've donned the outfit and won't take it off for weeks because, you see, this is not a "costume" at all, it's an *identity*. Sure, one pant leg is tucked into my boot and the other is hanging out, but that only adds to my "fresh off the trail" persona. My thumbs are tucked inside my gun belt and my chest is out because I am armed and dangerous. Bad guys beware: This town's not big enough for the both of us.

Capes and swords, camouflage, bandannas and six-shooters — these are the *uniforms* of boyhood. Little boys yearn to know they are powerful, they are dangerous, they are someone to be reckoned with. How many parents have tried in vain to prevent little Timmy from playing with guns? Give it up. If you do not supply a boy with weapons, he will make them from whatever materials are at hand. My boys chew their graham crackers into the shape of hand guns at the breakfast table. Every stick or fallen branch is a spear, or better, a bazooka. Despite what many modern educators would say, this is not a psychological disturbance brought on by violent television or chemical imbalance. Aggression is part of the masculine *design;* we are hardwired for it. If we believe that man is made in the image of God, then we would do well to remember that "the LORD is a warrior, the LORD is his name" (Ex. 15:3).

Little girls do not invent games where large numbers of people die, where bloodshed is a prerequisite for having fun. Hockey, for example, was not a feminine creation. Nor was boxing. A boy wants to attack something — and so does a man, even if it's only a little white ball on a tee. He wants to whack it into kingdom come. On the other hand, my boys do not sit down to tea parties. They do not call their friends on the phone to talk about relationships. They grow bored of games that have no element of danger or competition or bloodshed. Cooperative games based on "relational interdependence" are complete nonsense. "No one is killed?" they ask, incredulous. "No one wins? What's the point?" The universal nature of this ought to have convinced us by now: The boy is a warrior, the boy is his name. And those are not boyish antics he is doing. When boys play at war they are rehearsing their part in a much bigger drama. One day, you just might need that boy to defend you.

Those Union soldiers who charged the stone walls at Bloody Angle; the Allied troops that hit the beaches at Normandy or the sands of Iwo Jima — what would they have done without this deep part of their heart? Life *needs* a man to be fierce — and fiercely devoted. The wounds he will take throughout his life will cause him to lose heart if all he has been trained to be is soft. This is especially true in the murky waters of relationships, where a man feels least prepared to advance. As Bly says, "In every relationship something *fierce* is needed once in a while."

Now, this longing may have submerged from years of neglect, and a man may not feel that he is up to the battles he knows await him. Or it may have taken a very dark turn, as it has with inner-city gangs. But the desire is there. Every man wants to play the hero. Every man *needs* to know that he is powerful. Women didn't make *Braveheart* one of the best-selling films of the decade. *Flying Tigers*, *The Bridge on the River Kwai*, *The Magnificent Seven*, *Shane*, *High Noon*, *Saving Private Ryan*, *Top Gun*, the *Die Hard* films, *Gladiator* — the movies a man loves reveal what his heart longs for, what is set inside him from the day of his birth.

Like it or not, there is something fierce in the heart of every man.

AN ADVENTURE TO LIVE

"My mother loves to go to Europe on her vacations." We were talking about our love of the West, a friend and I, and why he moved out here from the East Coast. "And that's okay for her, I guess. There's a lot of culture there. But I need wildness." Our conversation was stirred by the film *Legends of the Fall*, the story of three young men coming of age in the early 1900s on their father's ranch in Montana. Alfred, the eldest, is practical, pragmatic, cautious. He heads off to the Big City to become a businessman and eventually, a politician. Yet something inside him dies. He becomes a hollow man. Samuel, the youngest, is still a boy in many ways, a tender child — literate, sensitive, timid. He is killed early in the film and we know he was not ready for battle.

Then there is Tristan, the middle son. He is wild at heart. It is Tristan who embodies the West — he catches and breaks the wild stallion, fights the grizzly with a knife, and wins the beautiful woman. I have yet to meet a man who wants to be Alfred or Samuel. I've yet to meet a woman who wants to marry one. There's a reason the American cowboy has taken on mythic proportions. He embodies a yearning every man knows from very young — to "go West," to find a place where he can be all he knows he was meant to be. To borrow Walter Brueggeman's description of God: "wild, dangerous, unfettered and free."

Now, let me stop for a moment and make something clear. I am no great white hunter. I have no dead animals adorning the walls of my house. I didn't play college football. In fact, in college I weighed 135 pounds and wasn't much of an athlete. Despite my childhood dreams, I have never been a race car driver or a fighter pilot. I have no interest in televised sports, I don't like cheap beer, and though I do drive an old jeep its tires are not ridiculously large. I say this because I anticipate that many readers — good men and women — will be tempted to dismiss this as some sort of macho-man pep rally. Not at all. I am simply searching, as many men (and hopeful women) are, for an authentic masculinity.

When winter fails to provide an adequate snow base, my boys bring their sleds in the house and ride them down the stairs. Just the other day, my wife found them with a rope out their second-story bedroom window, preparing to rappel down the side of the house. The recipe for fun is pretty simple raising boys: Add to any activity an element of danger, stir in a little exploration, add a dash of destruction, and you've got yourself a winner. The way they ski is a perfect example. Get to the top of the highest run, point your skis straight downhill and go, the faster the better. And this doesn't end with age, the stakes simply get higher.

A judge in his sixties, a real southern gentleman with a pinstriped suit and an elegant manner of speech, pulled me aside during a conference. Quietly, almost apologetically, he spoke of his love for sailing, for the open sea, and how he and a buddy eventually built their own boat. Then came a twinkle in his eye. "We were sailing off the coast of Bermuda a few years ago, when we were hit by a northeaster (a raging storm). Really, it came up out of nowhere. Twenty-foot swells in a thirty-foot homemade boat. I thought we were all going to die." A pause for dramatic effect, and then he confessed, "It was the best time of my life."

Compare your experience watching the latest James Bond or Indiana Jones thriller with, say, going to Bible study. The guaranteed success of each new release makes it clear — adventure is written into the heart of a man. And it's not just about having "fun." Adventure *requires* something of us, puts us to the test. Though we may fear the test, at the same time we yearn to be tested, to discover that we have what it takes. That's why we set off down the Snake River against all sound judgment, why a buddy and I pressed on through grizzly country to find good fishing, why I went off to Washington, D.C., as a young man to see if I could make it in those shark-infested waters. If a man has lost this desire, says he doesn't want it, that's only because he doesn't know he has what it takes, believes that he will fail the test. And so he decides it's better not to try. For reasons I hope to make clear later, most men hate the unknown and, like Cain, want to settle down and build their own city, get on top of their life.

But you can't escape it — there is something wild in the heart of every man.

A BEAUTY TO RESCUE

Romeo has his Juliet, King Arthur fights for Guinevere, Robin rescues Maid Marian, and I will never forget the first time I kissed my grade school sweetheart. It was in the fall of my seventh-grade year. I met Debbie in drama class, and fell absolutely head over heels. It was classic puppy love: I'd wait for

34

her after rehearsals were over, carry her books back to her locker. We passed notes in class, talked on the phone at night. I had never paid girls much attention, really, until now. This desire awakens a bit later in a boy's journey to manhood, but when it does his universe turns on its head. Anyway, I longed to kiss her but just couldn't work up the courage — until the last night of the school play. The next day was summer vacation, she was going away, and I knew it was now or never. Backstage, in the dark, I slipped her a quick kiss and she returned a longer one. Do you remember the scene from the movie *E.T.*, where the boy flies across the moon on his bike? Though I rode my little Schwinn home that night, I'm certain I never touched the ground.

There is nothing so inspiring to a man as a beautiful woman. She'll make you want to charge the castle, slay the giant, leap across the parapets. Or maybe, hit a home run. One day during a Little League game, my son Samuel was so inspired. He likes baseball, but most boys starting out aren't sure they really have it in them to be a great player. Sam's our firstborn, and like so many firstborns he is cautious. He always lets a few pitches go by before he takes a swing, and when he does, it's never a full

35

swing; every one of his hits up till this point were in the infield. Anyway, just as Sam steps up to bat this one afternoon, his friend from down the street, a cute little blonde girl, shows up along the first-base line. Standing up on tiptoe she yells out his name and waves to Sam. Pretending he doesn't notice her, he broadens his stance, grips the bat a little tighter, looks at the pitcher with something fierce in his eye. First one over the plate he knocks into center field.

A man wants to be the hero to the beauty. Young men going off to war carry a photo of their sweetheart in their wallet. Men who fly combat missions will paint a beauty on the side of their aircraft; the crews of the WWII B-17 bomber gave those flying fortresses names like *Me and My Gal* or the *Memphis Belle*. What would Robin Hood or King Arthur be without the woman they love? Lonely men fighting lonely battles. Indiana Jones and James Bond just wouldn't be the same without a beauty at their side, and inevitably they must fight for her. You see, it's not just that a man needs a battle to fight; he needs someone to fight *for*. Remember Nehemiah's words to the few brave souls defending a wall-less Jerusalem? "Don't be afraid . . . fight for your brothers, your sons and your daughters, your wives and your homes." The battle itself is never enough; a man yearns for romance. It's not enough to be a hero; it's that he is a hero *to someone* in particular, to the woman he loves. Adam was given the wind and the sea, the horse and the hawk, but as God himself said, things were just not right until there was Eve.

Yes, there is something passionate in the heart of every man.

THE FEMININE HEART

There are also three desires that I have found essential to a woman's heart, which are not entirely different from a man's and yet they remain distinctly feminine. Not every woman wants a battle to fight, but every woman yearns to be fought *for.* Listen to the longing of a woman's heart: She wants to be more than noticed — she wants to be *wanted.* She wants to be pursued. "I just want to be a priority to someone," a friend in her thirties told me. And her childhood dreams of a knight in shining armor coming to rescue her are not girlish fantasies; they are the core of the feminine heart and the life she knows she was made for. So Zach comes back for Paula in *An Officer and a Gentleman*, Frederick comes back for Jo in *Little Women*, and Edward returns to pledge his undying love for Eleanor in *Sense and Sensibility*.

Every woman also wants an adventure *to share*. One of my wife's favorite films is *The Man from Snowy River*. She loves the scene where Jessica, the beautiful young heroine, is rescued by Jim, her hero, and together they ride on horseback through the wilds of the Australian wilderness. "I want to be Isabo in *Ladyhawk*," confessed another female friend. "To be cherished, pursued, fought for — yes. But also, I want to be strong and a *part* of the adventure." So many men make the mistake of thinking that the woman *is* the adventure. But that is where the relationship immediately goes downhill. A woman doesn't want to be the adventure; she wants to be caught up into something greater than herself. Our friend went on to say, "I know myself and I know I'm not the adventure. So when a man makes me the point, I grow bored immediately. I know that story. Take me into one I don't know."

And finally, every woman wants to have a beauty to unveil. Not to conjure, but to unveil. Most women feel the pressure to be beautiful from very young, but that is not what I speak of. There is also a deep desire to simply and truly *be* the beauty, and be delighted in. Most little girls will remember playing dress up, or wedding day, or "twirling skirts," those flowing dresses that were perfect for spinning around in. She'll put her pretty dress on, come into the living room and twirl. What she longs for is to capture her daddy's delight. My wife remembers standing on top of the coffee table as a girl of five or six, and singing her heart out. *Do you see me?* asks the heart of every girl. *And are you captivated by what you see?*

The world kills a woman's heart when it tells her to be tough, efficient, and independent. Sadly, Christianity has missed her heart as well. Walk into most churches in America, have a look around, and ask yourself this question: What is a Christian woman? Again, don't listen to what is said, look at what you find there. There is no doubt about it. You'd have to admit a Christian woman is . . . tired. All we've offered the feminine soul is pressure to "be a good servant." No one is fighting for her heart, there is no grand adventure to be swept up in, and every woman doubts very much that she has any beauty to unveil.

Which would you rather be said of you: "Harry? Sure I know him. He's a real sweet guy." Or, "Yes, I know about Harry. He's a dangerous man . . . in a really good way." Ladies, how about you? Which man would you rather have as your mate? (Some women, hurt by masculinity gone bad, might argue for the "safe" man . . . and then wonder why, years later, there is no passion in their marriage, why he is distant and cold.) And as for your own femininity, which would you rather have said of you — that you are a "tireless worker," or that you are a "captivating woman"? I rest my case.

What if? What if those deep desires in our hearts are telling us the truth, revealing to us the life we were *meant* to live? God gave us eyes so that we might see; he gave us ears that we might hear; he gave us wills that we might choose, and he gave us hearts that we might *live*. The way we handle the heart is everything. A man must *know* he is powerful; he must *know* he has what it takes. A woman must *know* she is beautiful; she must *know* she is worth fighting for. "But you don't understand," said one woman to me. "I'm living with a hollow man." No, it's in there. His heart is there. It may have evaded you, like a wounded animal, always out of reach, one step beyond your catching. But it's there. "I don't know when I died," said another man. "But I feel like I'm just using up oxygen." I understand. Your heart may feel dead and gone, but it's there. Something wild and strong and valiant, just waiting to be released.

And so this is not a book about the seven things a man ought to do to be a nicer guy. It is a book about the recovery and release of a man's heart, his passions, his true nature, which he has been given by God. It's an invitation to rush the fields at Bannockburn, to go West, to leap from the falls and save the beauty. For if you are going to know who you truly are *as a man*, if you are going to find a life worth living, if you are going to love a woman deeply and not pass on your confusion to your children, you simply must get your heart back. You must head up into the high country of the soul, into wild and uncharted regions and track down that elusive prey.

Chapter Two

THE WILD ONE WHOSE IMAGE WE BEAR

How would telling people to be nice to one another get a man crucified? What government would execute Mister Rogers or Captain Kangaroo?

— PHILIP YANCEY

Safe? Who said anything about safe? 'Course he isn't safe. But he's good.

— C. S. LEWIS

This is a stem
Of that victorious stock, and let us fear
The native mightiness and fate of him.
— HENRY V

Remember that little guy I told you about, with the shiny boots and a pair of six-shooters? The best part of the story is that it wasn't all pretend. I had a place to live out those dreams. My grandfather, my father's father, was a cowboy. He worked his own cattle ranch in eastern Oregon, between the desert sage and the Snake River. And though I was raised in the suburbs, the redemption of my life and the real training grounds for my own masculine journey took place on that ranch, where I spent my boyhood summers. Oh, that every boy should be so lucky. To have your days filled with tractors and pickup trucks, horses and roping steers, running through the fields, fishing in the ponds. I was Huck Finn for three wonderful months every year. How I loved it when my grandfather — "Pop" is what I called him — would look at me, his thumbs tucked in his belt, smile, and say, "Saddle up."

One afternoon Pop took me into town, to my favorite store. It was a combination feed and tack/hardware/ranch supply shop. The classic dry goods store of the Old West, a wonderland of tools and equipment, saddles, bridles and blankets, fishing gear, pocketknives, rifles. It smelled of hay and linseed oil, of leather and gunpowder and kerosene — all the things that thrill a boy's

43

heart. That summer Pop was having a problem with an overrun pigeon population on the ranch. He hated the dirty birds, feared they were carrying diseases to the cattle. "Flying rats," is what he called them. Pop walked straight over to the firearms counter, picked out a BB rifle and a quart-sized milk carton with about a million BBs in it, and handed them to me. The old shop-keeper looked a bit surprised as he stared down at me, squinting over his glasses. "Isn't he a bit young for that?" Pop put his hand on my shoulder and smiled. "This is my grandson, Hal. He's riding shotgun for me."

WHERE DO WE COME FROM?

I may have walked into that feed store a squirrelly little kid, but I walked out as Sheriff Wyatt Earp, the Lone Ranger, Kit Carson. I had an identity and a place in the story. I was invited to be dangerous. If a boy is to become a man, if a man is to know he is one, this is not an option. A man *has* to know where he comes from, and what he's made of. One of the turning points in my good friend Craig's life — maybe *the* turning point — was the day he took back his father's name. Craig's father, Al McConnell, was

44

killed in the Korean War when Craig was only four months old. His mother remarried and Craig was adopted by his stepdad, a sour old navy captain who would call Craig a "seagull" whenever he was angry with him. Talk about an identity, a place in the story. He'd say, "Craig, you're nothing but a seagull — all you're good for is sitting, squawking, and . . ." (you get the idea).

When Craig was a man he learned the truth of his heritage — how his dad was a warrior who had been cut down in battle. How if he had lived, he was planning on going to the mission field, to take the gospel to a place no one else had ever gone before. Craig discovered that his real great-grandfather was William McConnell, the first missionary to Central America, a man who risked his life many times to bring Christ to a lost people. Craig changed his name to McConnell and with it took back a much more noble identity, a much more dangerous place in the story. Would that we were all so fortunate. Many men are ashamed of their fathers. "You're just like your father," is an arrow many a bitter mother fires at her son. Most of the men I know are trying hard *not* to become like their fathers. But who does that leave them to follow after? From whom will they derive their sense of strength?

Maybe it would be better to turn our search to the headwaters, to that mighty root from which these branches grow. Who is this One we allegedly come from, whose image every man bears? What is he like? In a man's search for his strength, telling him that he's made in the image of God may not sound like a whole lot of encouragement at first. To most men, God is either distant or he is weak — the very thing they'd report of their earthly fathers. Be honest now — what is your image of Jesus *as a man?* "Isn't he sort of meek and mild?" a friend remarked. "I mean, the pictures I have of him show a gentle guy with children all around. Kind of like Mother Teresa." Yes, those are the pictures I've seen myself in many churches. In fact, those are the *only* pictures I've seen of Jesus. As I've said before, they leave me with the impression that he was the world's nicest guy. Mister Rogers with a beard. Telling me to be like him feels like telling me to go limp and passive. Be nice. Be swell. Be like Mother Teresa.

I'd much rather be told to be like William Wallace.

BRAVEHEART INDEED

Wallace, if you'll recall, is the hero of the film *Braveheart*. He is the warrior poet who came as the liberator of Scotland in the early 1300s. When Wallace arrives on the scene, Scotland has been under the iron fist of English monarchs for centuries. The latest king is the worst of them all — Edward the Longshanks. A ruthless oppressor, Longshanks has devastated Scotland, killing her sons and raping her daughters. The Scottish nobles, supposed protectors of their flock, have instead piled heavy burdens on the backs of the people while they line their own purses by cutting deals with Longshanks. Wallace is the first to defy the English oppressors. Outraged, Longshanks sends his armies to the field of Sterling to crush the rebellion. The highlanders come down, in groups of hundreds and thousands. It's time for a showdown. But the nobles, cowards all, don't want a fight. They want a treaty with England that will buy them more lands and power. They are typical Pharisees, bureaucrats . . . religious administrators.

Without a leader to follow, the Scots begin to lose heart. One by one, then in larger numbers, they start to flee. At that moment Wallace rides in with his band of warriors, blue warpaint on their faces, ready for battle. Ignoring the nobles — who have gone to parley with the English captains to get another deal — Wallace goes straight for the hearts of the fearful Scots. "Sons of Scotland . . . you have come to fight as free men, and free men you are." He gives them an identity and a reason to fight. He reminds them that a life lived in fear is no life at all, that every last one of them will die some day. "And dying in your beds, many years from now, would you be willing to trade all the days from this day to that to come back here and tell our enemies that they may take our lives, but they'll never take our freedom!" He tells them they have what it takes. At the end of his stirring speech, the men are cheering. They are ready. Then Wallace's friend asks,

"Fine speech. Now what do we do?"
"Just be yourselves."
"Where are you going?"
"I'm going to pick a fight."

Finally, someone is going to stand up to the English tyrants. While the nobles jockey for position, Wallace rides out and interrupts the parley. He picks a fight with the English overlords and the Battle of Sterling ensues — a battle that begins the liberation of Scotland.

Now — is Jesus more like Mother Teresa or William Wallace? The answer is . . . it depends. If you're a leper, an outcast, a pariah of society whom no one has *ever* touched because you are "unclean," if all you have ever longed for is just one kind word, then Christ is the incarnation of tender mercy. He reaches out and touches you. On the other hand, if you're a Pharisee, one of those self-appointed doctrine police . . . watch out. On more than one occasion Jesus "picks a fight" with those notorious hypocrites. Take the story of the crippled woman in Luke 13. Here's the background: The Pharisees are like the Scottish nobles — they, too, load heavy burdens on the backs of God's people but do not lift a finger to help them. What is more, they are so bound to the Law that they insist it is a sin to heal someone on the Sabbath, for that would be doing "work." They have twisted God's intentions so badly they think that man was made for the Sabbath, rather than the Sabbath for man (Mark 2:27). Christ has already had a number of skirmishes with them, some over this very issue, leaving those quislings "wild with rage" (Luke 6:11 NLT).

Does Jesus tiptoe around the issue next time, so as not to "rock the boat" (the preference of so many of our leaders today)? Does he drop the subject in order to "preserve church unity"? Nope. He walks right into it, he baits them, he picks a fight. Let's pick up the story there:

> One Sabbath day as Jesus was teaching in a synagogue, he saw a woman who had been crippled by an evil spirit. She had been bent double for eighteen years and was unable to stand up straight. When Jesus saw her, he called her over and said, "Woman, you are healed of your sickness!" Then he touched her, and instantly she could stand straight. How she praised and thanked God! But the leader in charge of the synagogue was indignant that Jesus had healed her on the Sabbath day. "There are six days of the week for working," he said to the crowd. "Come on those days to be healed, not on the Sabbath." (Luke 13:10–14 NLT)

Can you believe this guy? What a weasel. Talk about completely missing the point. Christ is furious:

But the Lord replied, "You hypocrite!

You work on the Sabbath day! Don't you untie your ox or your donkey from their stalls on the Sabbath and lead them out for water? Wasn't it necessary for me, even on the Sabbath day, to free this dear woman from the bondage in which Satan has held her for eighteen years?" This shamed his enemies. And all the people rejoiced at the wonderful things he did. (Luke 13:15–17 NLT)

A BATTLE TO FIGHT

Christ draws the enemy out, exposes him for what he is, and shames him in front of everyone. The Lord is a *gentleman???* Not if you're in the service of his enemy. God has a battle to fight, and the battle is for our freedom. As Tremper Longman says, "Virtually every book of the Bible — Old and New Testaments — and almost every page tells us about God's warring activity." I wonder if the Egyptians who kept Israel under the whip would describe Yahweh as a Really Nice Guy? Plagues, pestilence, the death of every firstborn — that doesn't seem very gentlemanly now, does it? What would Miss Manners have to say about taking the promised land? Does wholesale slaughter fit under "Calling on Your New Neighbors"?

You remember that wild man, Samson? He's got a pretty impressive masculine résumé: killed a lion with his bare hands, pummeled and stripped thirty Philistines when they used his wife against him, and finally, after they burned her to death, he killed a thousand men with the jawbone of a donkey. Not a guy to mess with. But did you notice? All those events happened when *"the Spirit of the LORD* came upon him" (Judges 15:14, emphasis added). Now, let me make one thing clear: I am not advocating a sort of "macho man" image. I'm not suggesting we all head off to the gym and then to the beach to kick sand in the faces of wimpy Pharisees. I am attempting to rescue us from a very, very mistaken image we have of God — especially of Jesus — and therefore of men as his image-bearers. Dorothy Sayers wrote that the church has "very efficiently pared the claws of the Lion of Judah," making him "a fitting household pet for pale curates and pious old ladies." Is that the God you find in the Bible? To Job — who has questioned God's strength, he replies:

> Do you give the horse his strength
> or clothe his neck with a flowing
> mane?

Do you make him leap like a locust,
    striking terror with his proud
      snorting?
He paws fiercely, rejoicing in his
    strength,
    and charges into the fray.
He laughs at fear, afraid of nothing;
    he does not shy away from the
      sword.
The quiver rattles against his side,
    along with the flashing spear and
      lance.
In frenzied excitement he eats up the
    ground,
    he cannot stand still when the
      trumpet sounds.
At the blast of the trumpet he snorts,
    "Aha!"
    He catches the scent of battle from
      afar,
    the shout of commanders and the
      battle cry. (Job 39:19–25)

The war horse, the stallion, embodies the fierce heart of his Maker. And so do we; every man is "a stem of that victorious stock." Or at least, he was originally. You can tell what kind of man you've got simply by noting the impact he has on you. Does he make you bored? Does he scare you with his doctrinal nazism? Does he make you want to scream because he's just so very nice? In the Garden of Gesthemane, in the dead of night, a mob of thugs "carrying torches, lanterns and weapons" comes to take Christ away. Note the cowardice of it — why didn't they take him during the light of day, down in the town? Does Jesus shrink back in fear? No, he goes to face them head-on.

Jesus, knowing all that was going to happen to him, went out and asked them, "Who is it you want?"

"Jesus of Nazareth," they replied.

"I am he," Jesus said. (And Judas the traitor was standing there with them.) When Jesus said, "I am he," *they drew back and fell to the ground.*

Again he asked them, "Who is it you want?"

And they said, "Jesus of Nazareth."

"I told you that I am he," Jesus answered. "If you are looking for me, then let these men go." (John 18:4–8, emphasis added)

Talk about strength. The sheer force of Jesus' bold presence knocks the whole posse over. A few years ago a good man gave me a copy of a poem Ezra Pound wrote about

Christ, called "Ballad of the Goodly Fere."
It's become my favorite. Written from the
perspective of one of the men who followed
Christ, perhaps Simon Zelotes, it'll make a
lot more sense if you know that *fere* is an Old
English word that means *mate*, or *companion:*

Ha' we lost the goodliest fere o' all
For the priests and the gallows tree?
Aye lover he was of brawny men,
O' ships and the open sea.

When they came wi' a host to take Our
    Man
His smile was good to see,
"First let these go!" quo' our Goodly
    Fere,
"Or I'll see ye damned," says he.

Aye he sent us out through the crossed
    high spears
And the scorn of his laugh rang free,
"Why took ye not me when I walked
    about
Alone in the town?" says he.

Oh we drunk his "Hale" in the good
    red wine
When we last made company,

No capon priest was the Goodly Fere
But a man o' men was he.

I ha' seen him drive a hundred men
Wi' a bundle o' cords swung free,
That they took the high and holy house
For their pawn and treasury . . .

I ha' seen him cow a thousand men
On the hills o' Galilee.
They whined as he walked out calm
    between,
Wi' his eyes like the grey o' the sea,

Like the sea that brooks no voyaging
With the winds unleashed and free,
Like the sea that he cowed at Genseret
Wi' twey words spoke' suddenly.

A master of men was the Goodly Fere,
A mate of the wind and sea,
If they think they ha' slain our Goodly Fere
They are fools eternally.

Jesus is no "capon priest," no pale-faced
altar boy with his hair parted in the middle,
speaking softly, avoiding confrontation,
who at last gets himself killed because he
has no way out. He works with wood, com-
mands the loyalty of dockworkers. He is the

Lord of hosts, the captain of angel armies. And when Christ returns, he is at the head of a dreadful company, mounted on a white horse, with a double-edged sword, his robe dipped in blood (Rev. 19). Now that sounds a lot more like William Wallace than it does Mother Teresa.

No question about it — there is something fierce in the heart of God.

WHAT ABOUT ADVENTURE?

If you have any doubts as to whether or not God loves wildness, spend a night in the woods . . . alone. Take a walk out in a thunderstorm. Go for a swim with a pod of killer whales. Get a bull moose mad at you. Whose idea was this, anyway? The Great Barrier Reef with its great white sharks, the jungles of India with their tigers, the deserts of the Southwest with all those rattlesnakes — would you describe them as "nice" places? Most of the earth is not safe, but it's good. That struck me a little too late when hiking in to find the upper Kenai River in Alaska. My buddy Craig and I were after the salmon and giant rainbow trout that live in those icy waters. We were warned about bears, but didn't really take it seriously until we were deep into the woods. Grizzly sign was everywhere — salmon strewn about the trail, their heads bitten off. Piles of droppings the size of small dogs. Huge claw marks on the trees, about head-level. *We're dead,* I thought. *What are we doing out here?*

It then occurred to me that after God made all this, he pronounced it *good*, for heaven's sake. It's his way of letting us know he rather prefers adventure, danger, risk, the element of surprise. This whole creation is unapologetically *wild*. God loves it that way. But what about his own life? We know he has a battle to fight — but does God have an *adventure* to live? I mean, he already knows everything that's going to happen, right? How could there be any risk to his life; hasn't he got everything under absolute control?

In an attempt to secure the sovereignty of God, theologians have overstated their case and left us with a chess-player God playing both sides of the board, making all his moves and all ours too. But clearly, this is not so. God is a person who takes immense risks. No doubt the biggest risk of all was when he gave angels and men free will, including the freedom to reject him — not just once, but every single day. Does God cause a person to sin? "Absolutely not!" says Paul (Gal. 2:17). Then he can't be moving all the pieces on the board, because people sin all the time. Fallen angels and men use their powers to commit horrendous daily evil. Does God stop every bullet fired at an innocent victim? Does he prevent teenage liaisons from producing teenage pregnancies? There is something much more risky going on here than we're often willing to admit.

Most of us do everything we can to *reduce* the element of risk in our lives. We wear our seat belts, watch our cholesterol, and practice birth control. I know some couples who have decided against having children altogether; they simply aren't willing to chance the heartache children often bring. What if they are born with a crippling disease? What if they turn their backs on us, and God? What if . . . ? God seems to fly in the face of all caution. Even though he *knew* what would happen, what heartbreak and suffering and devastation would follow upon our disobedience, God chose to have children. And unlike some hyper-controlling parents, who take away every element of choice they can from their children, God gave us a remarkable choice. He did not *make* Adam and Eve obey him. He took a risk. A staggering risk, with staggering consequences. He let others into his story, and he lets their choices shape it profoundly.

This is the world he has made. This is the world that is still going on. And he doesn't walk away from the mess we've made of it. Now he lives, almost cheerfully, certainly heroically, in a dynamic relationship with us and with our world. "Then the Lord intervened" is perhaps the single most common phrase about him in Scripture, in one form or another. Look at the stories he writes. There's the one where the children of Israel are pinned against the Red Sea, no way out, with Pharaoh and his army barreling down on them in murderous fury. Then God shows up. There's Shadrach, Meshach, and Abednego, who get rescued only *after* they're thrown into the fiery furnace. Then God shows up. He lets the mob kill Jesus, bury him . . . then he shows up. Do you know why God loves writing such incredible stories? Because *he loves to come through*. He loves to show us that he has what it takes.

It's not the nature of God to limit his risks and cover his bases. Far from it. Most of the time, he actually lets the odds stack up against him. Against Goliath, a seasoned soldier and a trained killer, he sends . . . a freckle-faced little shepherd kid with a slingshot. Most commanders going into battle want as many infantry as they can get. God cuts Gideon's army from thirty-two thousand to three-hundred. Then he equips the ragtag little band that's left with torches and watering pots. It's not just a battle or two that God takes his chances with, either. Have you thought about his handling of the gospel? God needs to get a message out to the human race, without which they will perish . . . forever. What's the plan? First, he starts with the most unlikely group ever: a couple of prostitutes, a few fishermen with no better than a second-grade education, a tax collector. Then, he passes the ball to us. Unbelievable.

God's relationship with us and with our world is just that: a *relationship*. As with every relationship, there's a certain amount of unpredictability, and the ever-present likelihood that you'll get hurt. The ultimate risk anyone ever takes is to love, for as C. S. Lewis says, "Love anything and your heart will be wrung and possibly broken. If you want to make sure of keeping it intact you must give it to no one, not even an animal." But God does give it, again and again and again, until he is literally bleeding from it all. God's willingness to risk is just astounding — far beyond what any of us would do were we in his position.

Trying to reconcile God's sovereignty and man's free will has stumped the church for ages. We must humbly acknowledge that there's a great deal of mystery involved, but for those aware of the discussion, I am not advocating open theism. Nevertheless, there is definitely something wild in the heart of God.

A BEAUTY TO FIGHT FOR

And all his wildness and all his fierceness are inseparable from his romantic heart. That theologians have missed this says more about theologians than it does about God. Music, wine, poetry, sunsets . . . those were *his* inventions, not ours. We simply discovered what he had already thought of. Lovers and honeymooners choose places like Hawaii, the Bahamas, or Tuscany as a backdrop for their love. But whose idea was Hawaii, the Bahamas, and Tuscany? Let's bring this a little closer to home. Whose idea was it to create the human form in such a way that a kiss could be so delicious? And he didn't stop there, as only lovers know. Starting with her eyes, King Solomon is feasting on his beloved through the course of their wedding night. He loves her hair, her smile, her lips "drop sweetness as the honeycomb" and "milk and honey are under her tongue." You'll notice he's working his way *down:*

Your neck is like the tower of David,
   built with elegance . . .
Your two breasts are like two fawns . . .

Until the day breaks
   and the shadows flee
I will go to the mountain of myrrh
   and to the hill of incense. (Song 4:4–6)

And his wife responds by saying, "Let my lover come into his garden and taste its choice fruits" (Song 4:16). What kind of God would put the Song of Songs in the canon of Holy Scripture? Really, now, is it conceivable that such an erotic and scandalous book would have been placed in the Bible by the Christians *you* know? And what a delicate, poetic touch, "two fawns." This is no pornography, but there is no way to try to explain it all as "theological metaphor." That's just nonsense. In fact, God himself actually speaks in person in the Songs, once in the entire book. Solomon has taken his beloved to his bedchamber and the two are doing everything that lovers do there. God blesses it all, whispering, "Eat, O friends, and drink; drink your fill, O lovers" (Song 5:1), offering, as if needed, his own encouragement. And then he pulls the shades.

God is a romantic at heart, and he has his

own bride to fight for. He is a jealous lover, and his jealousy is for the hearts of his people and for their freedom. As Francis Frangipane so truly states, "Rescue is the constant pattern of God's activity."

For Zion's sake I will not keep silent,
     for Jerusalem's sake I will not remain quiet,
till her righteousness shines out like the
          dawn,
     her salvation like a blazing torch . . .

As a bridegroom rejoices over his bride,
     so will your God rejoice over you.
          (Isa. 62:1, 5)

And though she has committed adultery against him, though she has fallen captive to his enemy, God is willing to move heaven and earth to win her back. He will stop at nothing to set her free:

Who is this coming from Edom,
     from Bozrah, with his garments stained
          crimson?
Who is this, robed in splendor,
     striding forward in the greatness of his
          strength?
"It is I, speaking in righteousness,
     mighty to save."

Why are your garments red,
  like those of one treading the
    winepress?
"I have trodden the winepress alone;
  from the nations no one was with me.
I trampled them in my anger
  and trod them down in my wrath;
their blood spattered my garments,
  and I stained all my clothing.
For the day of vengeance was in my heart,
  and the year of my redemption has
    come. (Isa. 63:1–4)

Whoa. Talk about a Braveheart. This is one fierce, wild, and passionate guy. I have never heard Mister Rogers talk like that. Come to think of it, I have never heard anyone in church talk like that, either. But this is the God of heaven and earth. The Lion of Judah.

LITTLE BOYS AND LITTLE GIRLS

And this is our true Father, the stock from which the heart of man is drawn. Strong, courageous love. As George MacDonald wrote,

Thou art my life — I the brook, thou the spring.

65

Because thine eyes are open, I can see;
Because thou art thyself, 'tis therefore I
am me. (*Diary of an Old Soul*)

I've noticed that so often our word to boys is *don't*. Don't climb on that, don't break anything, don't be so aggressive, don't be so noisy, don't be so messy, don't take such crazy risks. But God's design — which he placed in boys as the picture of himself — is a resounding *yes*. Be fierce, be wild, be passionate. Now, none of this is to diminish the fact that a woman bears God's image as well. The masculine and feminine run throughout all creation. As Lewis says, "Gender is a reality and a more fundamental reality than sex . . . a fundamental polarity which divides all created beings." There is the sun and then there are the moon and stars; there is the rugged mountain and there is the field of wildflowers that grows upon it. A male lion is awesome to behold, but have you ever seen a lionness? There is also something wild in the heart of a woman, but it is feminine to the core, more *seductive* than fierce.

Eve and all her daughters are also "a stem of that victorious stock," but in a wonderfully different way. As a counselor and a friend, and especially as a husband, I've been honored to be welcomed into the deep heart of Eve. Often when I am with a woman, I find myself quietly wondering, *What is she telling me about God? I know he wants to say something to the world through Eve — what is it?* And after years of hearing the heart-cry of women, I am convinced beyond a doubt of this: God wants to be loved. He wants to be a priority to someone. How could we have missed this? From cover to cover, from beginning to end, the cry of God's heart is, "Why won't you choose Me?" It is amazing to me how humble, how *vulnerable* God is on this point. "You will . . . find me," says the Lord, "when you seek me with all your heart" (Jer. 29:13). In other words, "Look for me, pursue me — I want you to pursue me." Amazing. As Tozer says, "God waits to be wanted."

And certainly we see that God wants not merely an adventure, but an adventure to *share.* He didn't have to make us, but he *wanted* to. Though he knows the name of every star and his kingdom spans galaxies, God delights in being a part of our lives. Do you know why he often doesn't answer prayer right away? Because he wants to talk to us, and sometimes that's the only way to get us to stay and *talk* to him. His heart is for relationship, for shared adventure to the core.

And yes, God has a beauty to unveil. There's a reason that a man is captivated by a woman. Eve is the crown of creation. If you follow the Genesis narrative carefully, you'll see that each new stage of creation is better than the one before. First, all is formless, empty and dark. God begins to fashion the raw materials, like an artist working with a rough sketch or a lump of clay. Light and dark, land and sea, earth and sky — it's beginning to take shape. With a word, the whole floral kingdom adorns the earth. Sun, moon, and stars fill the sky. Surely and certainly, his work expresses greater detail and definition. Next come fish and fowl, porpoises and red-tailed hawks. The wild animals are next, all those amazing creatures. A trout is a wonderful creature, but a horse is truly magnificent. Can you hear the crescendo starting to swell, like a great symphony building and surging higher and higher?

Then comes Adam, the triumph of God's handiwork. It is not to any member of the animal kingdom that God says, "You are my very image, the icon of my likeness." Adam bears the likeness of God in his fierce, wild, and passionate heart. And yet, there is one more finishing touch. There is Eve. Creation comes to its high point, its climax with her. She is God's finishing touch. And all Adam can say is, "Wow." Eve embodies the beauty and the mystery and the tender vulnerability of God. As the poet William Blake said, "The naked woman's body is a portion of eternity too great for the eye of man."

The reason a woman wants a beauty to unveil, the reason she asks, *Do you delight in me?* is simply that God does as well. God is captivating beauty. As David prays, "One thing I ask of the LORD, this is what I seek: that I may . . . gaze upon the beauty of the LORD" (Ps. 27:4). Can there be any doubt that God wants to be *worshiped?* That he wants to be seen, and for us to be captivated by what we see? As C. S. Lewis wrote, "The beauty of the female is the root of joy to the female as well as to the male . . . to desire the enjoying of her own beauty is the obedience of Eve, and to both it is in the lover that the beloved tastes of her own delightfulness."

This is far too simple an outline, I admit. There is so much more to say, and these are not hard and rigid categories. A man needs to be tender at times, and a woman will sometimes need to be fierce. But if a man is only tender, we know something is deeply wrong, and if a woman is only fierce, we sense she is not what she was meant to be. If

you'll look at the essence of little boys and
little girls, I think you'll find I am not far
from my mark. Strength and beauty. As the
psalmist says,

> One thing God has spoken,
> two things have I heard:
> that you, O God, are strong,
> and that you, O Lord, are loving.
>   (Ps. 62:11–12)

Chapter Three

THE QUESTION THAT HAUNTS EVERY MAN

The tragedy of life is what dies inside a man while he lives.
— ALBERT SCHWEITZER

He begins to die, that quits his desires.
— GEORGE HERBERT

Are you there?
Say a prayer for the Pretender
Who started out so young and strong
Only to surrender.

— JACKSON BROWNE
"The Pretender"
(© 1976 by Swallow Turn Music)

Our local zoo had for years one of the biggest African lions I've ever seen. A huge male, nearly five hundred pounds, with a wonderful mane and absolutely enormous paws. *Panthera leo*. The King of the Beasts. Sure, he was caged, but I'm telling you the bars offered small comfort when you stood within six feet of something that in any other situation saw you as an easy lunch. Honestly, I felt I ought to shepherd my boys past him at a safe distance, as if he could pounce on us if he really wanted to. Yet he was my favorite, and whenever the others would wander on to the monkey house or the tigers, I'd double back just for a few more minutes in the presence of someone so powerful and noble and deadly. Perhaps it was fear mingled with admiration, perhaps it was simply that my heart broke for the big old cat.

This wonderful, terrible creature should have been out roaming the savanna, ruling his pride, striking fear into the heart of every wildebeest, bringing down zebras and gazelles whenever the urge seized him. Instead, he spent every hour of every day and every night of every year alone, in a cage smaller than your bedroom, his food served to him through a little metal door. Sometimes late at night, after the city had gone to sleep, I would hear his roar come down from the hills. It sounded not so much fierce, but rather mournful. During all of my visits, he never looked me in the eye. I desperately wanted him to, wanted for his sake the chance to stare me down, would have loved it if he took a swipe at me. But he just lay there, weary with that deep weariness that comes from boredom, taking shallow breaths, rolling now and then from side to side.

For after years of living in a cage, a lion no longer even believes it is a lion . . . and a man no longer believes he is a man.

THE LION OF JUDAH??

A man is fierce . . . passionate . . . wild at heart? You wouldn't know it from what normally walks around in a pair of trousers. If a man is the image of the Lion of Judah, how come there are so many lonely women, so many fatherless children, so few *men* around? Why is it that the world seems filled with "caricatures" of masculinity? There's the guy who lives behind us. He spends his entire weekend in front of the tube watching sports while his sons play outside — without him. We've lived here nine years and I think I've seen him play with his boys maybe twice. What's with that? Why won't he *engage?* And

73

the guy the next street over, who races motorcycles and drives a huge truck and wears a leather jacket and sort of swaggers when he walks. I thought James Dean died years ago. What's with him? It looks manly, but it seems cartoonish, overdone.

How come when men look in their hearts they don't discover something valiant and dangerous, but instead find anger, lust, and fear? Most of the time, I feel more fearful than I do fierce. Why is that? It was one hundred and fifty years ago that Thoreau wrote, "The mass of men lead lives of quiet desperation," and it seems nothing has changed. As the line from *Braveheart* has it, "All men die; few men ever really live." And so most women lead lives of quiet resignation, having given up on their hope for a true man.

The real life of the average man seems a universe away from the desires of his heart. There is no battle to fight, unless it's traffic and meetings and hassles and bills. The guys who meet for coffee every Thursday morning down at the local coffee shop and share a few Bible verses with each other — where is their great battle? And the guys who hang out down at the bowling alley, smoking and having a few too many — they're in the exact same place. The swords

74

and castles of their boyhood have long been replaced with pencils and cubicles; the six-shooters and cowboy hats laid aside for minivans and mortgages. The poet Edwin Robinson captured the quiet desperation this way:

> Miniver Cheevy, child of scorn,
> Grew lean while he assailed the
>   seasons;
> He wept that he was ever born
> And he had reasons.
>
> Miniver loved the days of old
> When swords were bright and steeds
>   were prancing;
> The vision of a warrior bold
> Would set him dancing.
>
> Miniver Cheevy, born too late,
> Scratched his head and kept on
>   thinking;
> Miniver coughed, and called it fate,
> And kept on drinking. ("Miniver
>   Cheevy")

Without a great battle in which a man can live and die, the fierce part of his nature goes underground and sort of simmers there in a sullen anger that seems to have no reason. A few weeks ago I was on a flight to the West Coast. It was dinnertime, and right in the middle of the meal the guy in front of me drops his seat back as far as it can go, with a couple of hard shoves back at me to make sure. I wanted to knock him into First Class. A friend of mine is having trouble with his toy shop, because the kids who come in "tick him off" and he's snapping at them. Not exactly good for business. So many men, good men, confess to losing it at their own children regularly. Then there's the guy in front of me at a stoplight yesterday. It turned green, but he didn't move; I guess he wasn't paying attention. I gave a little toot on my horn to draw his attention to the fact that now there were twenty-plus cars piling up behind us. The guy was out of his car in a flash, yelling threats, ready for a fight. Truth be told, I wanted desperately to meet him there. Men are angry, and we really don't know why.

And how come there are so many "sports widows," losing their husbands each weekend to the golf course or the TV? Why are so many men addicted to sports? It's the biggest adventure many of them ever taste. Why do so many others lose themselves in their careers? Same reason. I noticed the other day that the *Wall Street Journal* advertises itself to men as "adventures in capitalism." I know guys who spend hours on-line, e-trading stocks. There's a taste of excitement and risk to it, no question. And who's to blame them? The rest of their life is chores and tedious routine. It's no coincidence that many men fall into an affair not for love, not even for sex, but, by their own admission, for adventure. So many guys have been told to put that adventurous spirit behind them and "be responsible," meaning, live only for duty. All that's left are pictures on the wall of days gone by, and maybe some gear piled in the garage. Ed Sissman writes,

> Men past forty
> Get up nights, Look out at city lights
> And wonder
> Where they made the wrong turn
> And why life is so long.

I hope you're getting the picture by now. If a man does not find those things for which his heart is made, if he is never even invited to live for them from his deep heart, he will look for them in some other way. Why is pornography the number one snare for men? He longs for the beauty, but without his fierce and passionate heart he cannot find her or win her or keep her. Though he is powerfully drawn to the woman, he does not know how to fight for her or even that he *is* to fight for her. Rather, he finds her mostly a mystery that he knows he cannot solve and so at a soul level he keeps his distance. And privately, secretly, he turns to the imitation. What makes pornography so addictive is that more than anything else in a lost man's life, it makes him *feel* like a man without ever requiring a thing of him. The less a guy feels like a real man in the presence of a real woman, the more vulnerable he is to porn.

And so a man's heart, driven into the darker regions of the soul, denied the very things he most deeply desires, comes out in darker places. Now, a man's struggles, his wounds and addictions, are a bit more involved than that, but those are the core reasons. As the poet George Herbert warned, "he begins to die, that quits his desires." And you know what? We all know it. Every man knows that something's happened, something's gone wrong . . . we just don't know what it is.

OUR FEAR

I spent ten years of my life in the theater, as an actor and director. They were, for the most part, joyful years. I was young and energetic and pretty good at what I did. My wife was part of the theater company I managed, and we had many close friends there. I tell you this so that you will understand what I am about to reveal. In spite of the fact that my memories of theater are nearly all happy ones, I keep having this recurring nightmare. This is how it goes: I suddenly find myself in a theater — a large, Broadway-style playhouse, the kind every actor aspires to play. The house lights are low and the stage lights full, so from my position onstage I can barely make out the audience, but I sense it is a full house. Standing room only. So far, so good. Actors love playing to a full house. But I am not loving the moment at all. I am paralyzed with fear. A play is under way and I've got a crucial part. But I have no idea what play it is. I don't know what part I'm supposed to be playing; I don't know my lines; I don't even know my cues.

This is every man's deepest fear: to be exposed, to be found out, to be discovered as an impostor, and not really a man. The dream has nothing to do with acting; that's just the context for my fear. You have yours. A man bears the image of God in his strength, not so much physically but soulfully. Regardless of whether or not he knows the biblical account, if there's one thing a man does know he knows he is made to *come through.* Yet he wonders . . . *Can I? Will I?* When the going gets rough, when it really matters, will he pull it off? For years my soul lived in this turmoil. I'd often wake in the morning with an anxiousness that had no immediate source. My stomach was frequently tied in knots. One day my dear friend Brent asked, "What do you do now that you don't act anymore?" I realized at that moment that my whole life felt like a performance, like I am always "on." I felt in every situation that I must prove myself again. After I spoke or taught a class, I'd hang on what others would say, hoping they would say it went well. Each counseling session felt like a new test: *Can I come through, again? Was my last success all that I had?*

One of my clients got a great promotion and a raise. He came in depressed. *Good grief,* I thought. *Why?* Every man longs to be praised, and paid well on top of it. He confessed that although the applause felt great, he knew it only set him up for a bigger fall. Tomorrow, he'd have to do it all over, hit the ball out of the park again. Every man feels that the world is asking him to be something he doubts very much he has it in him to be. This is universal; I have yet to meet an honest man who won't admit it. Yes, there are many dense men who are wondering what I'm talking about; for them, life is fine and they are doing great. Just wait. Unless it's really and truly a reflection of genuine strength, it's a house of cards, and it'll come down sooner or later. Anger will surface, or an addiction. Headaches, an ulcer, or maybe an affair.

Honestly — how do you see yourself as a man? Are words like *strong, passionate,* and *dangerous* words you would choose? Do you have the courage to ask those in your life what *they* think of you as a man? What words do you fear they would choose? I mentioned the film *Legends of the Fall,* how every man who's seen it wants to be Tristan. But most see themselves as Alfred or Samuel. I've talked to many men about the film *Braveheart* and though every single one of them would love to be William Wallace, the dangerous warrior-hero, most see themselves as Robert the Bruce, the weak, intimidated guy who keeps folding under pressure. I'd love to think of myself as Indiana Jones; I'm afraid I'm more like Woody Allen.

The comedian Garrison Keillor wrote a very funny essay on this in his *The Book of Guys*. Realizing one day that he was not being honest about himself as a man, he sat down to make a list of his strengths and weaknesses:

USEFUL THINGS I CAN DO:

Be nice.

Make a bed.

Dig a hole.

Write books.

Sing alto or bass.

Read a map.

Drive a car.

USEFUL THINGS I CAN'T DO:

Chop down big trees and cut them into lumber or firewood.

Handle a horse, train a dog, or tend a herd of animals.

Handle a boat without panicking the others.

Throw a fastball, curve, or slider.

Load, shoot, and clean a gun. Or bow and arrow. Or use either of them, or a spear, net, snare, boomerang, or blowgun, to obtain meat.

Defend myself with my bare hands.

Keillor confesses: "Maybe it's an okay report card for a *person* but I don't know any persons . . . For a guy, it's not good. A woman would go down the list and say, 'What does it matter if a guy can handle a boat? Throw a curveball? Bag a deer? Throw a left hook? This is 1993.' But that's a womanly view of manhood." Craig and I were joking about this as we hacked our way through grizzly-infested woods in Alaska. The only other guys we met all day were a group of locals on their way out. They looked like something out of *Soldier of Fortune* magazine — sawed-off shotguns, pistols, bandoleers of ammo slung across their chests, huge knives. They were ready. They had what it takes. And we? We had a whistle. I'm serious. That's what we brought for our dangerous trek through the wild: a whistle. Talk about a couple of pansies. Craig confessed, "Me — what can I really do? I mean really? I know how to operate a fax machine."

That's how most men feel about their readiness to fight, to live with risk, to capture the beauty. We have a whistle. You see, even though the *desires* are there for a battle to fight, an adventure to live, and a beauty to rescue, even though our boyhood dreams once were filled with those things, we don't think we're up to it. Why don't men play the man? Why don't they offer their strength to a world desperately in need of it? For two simple reasons: We doubt very much that we have any real strength to offer, and we're pretty certain that if we did offer what we have it wouldn't be enough. Something has gone wrong and we know it.

What's happened to us? The answer is partly back in the story of mankind, and partly in the details of each man's story.

WHAT IS A MAN FOR?

Why does God create Adam? What is a man for? If you know what something is designed to do, then you know its purpose in life. A retriever loves the water; a lion loves the hunt; a hawk loves to soar. It's what they're made for. Desire reveals design, and design reveals destiny. In the case of human beings, our design is also revealed by our desires. Let's take adventure. Adam and all his sons after him are given an incredible mission: rule and subdue, be fruitful and multiply. "Here is the entire earth, Adam. Explore it, cultivate it, care for it — it is your kingdom." Whoa . . . talk about an invitation. This is permission to do a heck of a lot more than cross the street. It's a charter to find the equator; it's a commission to build Camelot. Only Eden is a garden at that point; everything else is wild, so far as we know. No river has been charted, no ocean crossed, no mountain climbed. No one's discovered the molecule, or fuel injection, or Beethoven's Fifth. It's a blank page, waiting to be written. A clean canvas, waiting to be painted.

Most men think they are simply here on earth to kill time — and it's killing them. But the truth is precisely the opposite. The secret longing of your heart, whether it's to build a boat and sail it, to write a symphony and play it, to plant a field and care for it — those are the things you were made to do. That's what you're here for. Explore, build, conquer — you don't have to tell a boy to do those things for the simple reason that it *is his purpose*. But it's going to take risk, and danger, and there's the catch. Are we willing to live with the level of risk God invites us to? Something inside us hesitates.

Let's take another desire — why does a man long for a battle to fight? Because when we enter the story in Genesis, we step into a world at war. The lines have already been drawn. Evil is waiting to make its next move. Somewhere back before Eden, in the mystery of eternity past, there was a coup, a rebellion, an assassination attempt. Lucifer, the prince of angels, the captain of the guard, rebelled against the Trinity. He tried to take the throne of heaven by force, assisted by a third of the angelic army, in whom he instilled his own malice. They failed, and were hurled from the presence of the Trinity. But they were not destroyed, and the battle is not over. God now has an enemy . . . and so do we. Man is not born into a sitcom or a soap opera; he is born into a world at war. This is not *Home Improvement*; it's *Saving Private Ryan*. There will be many, many battles to fight on many different battlefields.

And finally, why does Adam long for a beauty to rescue? Because there is Eve. He is going to need her, and she is going to need him. In fact, Adam's first and greatest battle is just about to break out, as a battle for Eve. But let me set the stage a bit more. Before Eve is drawn from Adam's side and leaves that ache that never goes away until he is with her, God gives Adam some instructions on the care of creation, and his role in the unfolding story. It's pretty basic, and very generous. "You may freely eat any fruit in the garden except fruit from the tree of the knowledge of good and evil" (Gen. 2:16–17 NLT). Okay, most of us have heard about that. But notice what God *doesn't* tell Adam.

There is no warning or instruction over what is about to occur: the Temptation of Eve. This is just staggering. Notably missing from the dialogue between Adam and God is something like this: "Adam, one more thing. A week from Tuesday, about four in the afternoon, you and Eve are going to be down in the orchard and something dangerous is going to happen. Adam, are you listening? The eternal destiny of the human race hangs on this moment. Now, here's what I want you to do . . ." he doesn't tell him. He doesn't even mention it, so far as we know. Good grief — *why not?!* Because God *believes* in Adam. This is what he's designed to do — to come through in a pinch. Adam doesn't need play-by-play instructions because this is what Adam is *for*. It's already there, everything he needs, in his design, in his heart.

Needless to say, the story doesn't go well. Adam fails; he fails Eve, and the rest of humanity. Let me ask you a question: Where is Adam, while the serpent is tempting Eve? He's standing right there: "She also gave some to her husband, who was with her. Then he ate it, too" (Gen. 3:6 NLT). The Hebrew for "with her" means right there, elbow to elbow. Adam isn't away in another part of the forest; he has no alibi. He is standing right there, watching the whole thing unravel. What does he do? Nothing. Absolutely nothing. He says not a word, doesn't lift a finger.* He won't risk, he won't fight, and he won't rescue Eve. Our first father — the first real man — gave in to paralysis. He denied his very nature and went passive. And every man after him, every son of Adam, carries in his heart now the same failure. Every man repeats the sin of Adam, every day. We won't risk, we won't fight, and we won't rescue Eve. We truly are a chip off the old block.

Lest we neglect Eve, I must point out that

*I'm indebted to Crabb, Hudson, and Andrews for pointing this out in *The Silence of Adam*.

she fails her design as well. Eve is given to Adam as his *ezer kenegdo* — or as many translations have it, his "help meet" or "helper." Doesn't sound like much, does it? It makes me think of Hamburger Helper. But Robert Alter says this is "a notoriously difficult word to translate." It means something far more powerful than just "helper"; it means *"lifesaver."* The phrase is only used elsewhere of God, when you need him to come through for you desperately. "There is no one like the God of Jeshurun, who rides on the heavens to help you" (Deut. 33:26). Eve is a life giver, she is Adam's ally. It is to *both* of them that the charter for adventure is given. It will take both of them to sustain life. And they will both need to fight together.

Eve is deceived . . . and rather easily, as my friend Jan Meyers points out. In *The Allure of Hope*, Jan says, "Eve was convinced that God was withholding something from her." Not even the extravagance of Eden could convince her that God's heart is good. "When Eve was [deceived], the artistry of being a woman took a fateful dive into the barren places of control and loneliness." Now every daughter of Eve wants to "control her surrounding, her relationships, her God." No longer is she vulnerable, now she

89

will be grasping. No longer does she want simply to share in the adventure; now, she wants to control it. And as for her beauty, she either hides it in fear and anger, or she uses it to secure her place in the world. "In our fear that no one will speak on our behalf or protect us or fight for us, we start to re-create both ourselves and our role in the story. We manipulate our surroundings so we don't feel so defenseless." Fallen Eve either becomes rigid or clingy. Put simply, Eve is no longer simply *inviting*. She is either hiding in busyness or demanding that Adam come through for her; usually, an odd combination of both.

POSERS

Adam knows now that he has blown it, that something has gone wrong within him, that he is no longer what he was meant to be. Adam doesn't just make a bad decision; he *gives away* something essential to his nature. He is marred now, his strength is fallen, and he knows it. Then what happens? Adam hides. "I was afraid because I was naked; so I hid" (Gen. 3:10). You don't need a course in psychology to understand men. Understand that verse, let its implications sink in, and the men around you will suddenly come into focus. We are hiding, every last one of us. Well aware that we, too, are not what we were meant to be, desperately afraid of exposure, terrified of being seen for what we are and *are not,* we have run off into the bushes. We hide in our office, at the gym, behind the newspaper and mostly *behind our personality.* Most of what you encounter when you meet a man is a facade, an elaborate fig leaf, a brilliant disguise.

Driving back from dinner one night, a friend and I were just sort of shooting the breeze about life and marriage and work. As the conversation deepened, he began to admit some of the struggles he was having. Then he came out with this confession: "The truth is, John, I feel like I'm just [bluffing] my way through life . . . and that someday soon I'll be exposed as an impostor." I was so surprised. This is a popular, successful guy who most people like the moment they meet him. He's bright, articulate, handsome, and athletic. He's married to a beautiful woman, has a great job, drives a new truck, and lives in a big house. There is nothing on the outside that says, "not really a man." But inside, it's another story. It always is.

Before I ever mentioned my nightmare about being onstage with nothing to say, another friend shared with me that he, too, is having a recurring nightmare. It involves a murder, and the FBI. Apparently, in his dream, he has killed someone and buried the body out back of his house. But the authorities are closing in, and he knows that any moment they'll discover the crime scene and he'll be caught. The dream always ends just before he is found out. He wakes in a cold sweat. "Any day now, I'll be found out" is a pretty common theme among us guys. Truth be told, most of us are faking our way through life. We pick only those battles we are sure to win, only those adventures we are sure to handle, only those beauties we are sure to rescue.

Let me ask the guys who don't know much about cars: How do you talk to your mechanic? I know a bit about fixing cars, but not much, and when I'm around my mechanic I feel like a weenie. So what do I do? I fake it; I pose. I assume a sort of casual, laid-back manner I imagine "the guys" use when hanging around the lunch truck, and I wait for him to speak. "Looks like it might be your fuel mixture," he says. "Yeah, I thought it might be that." "When was the last time you had your carb rebuilt?" "Oh I dunno . . . it's probably been years." (I'm guessing he's talking about my carburetor, and I have no idea if it's ever been rebuilt.) "Well, we'd better do it now or you're going to end up on some country road miles from nowhere and then you'll have to do it yourself." "Yeah," I say casually, as if I don't want to be bothered having to rebuild that thing even though I know I wouldn't have the slightest idea where to begin. All I have is a whistle, remember? I tell him to go ahead, and he sticks out his hand, a big, greasy hand that says *I know tools real well* and what am I supposed to do? I'm dressed in a coat and tie because I'm supposed to give a talk at some women's luncheon, but I can't say, "Gee, I'd rather not get my hands dirty," so I take his hand and pump it extra hard.

Or how about you fellas who work in the corporate world: How do you act in the boardroom, when the heat is on? What do you say when the Big Boss is riding you hard? "Jones, what the devil is going on down there in your division? You guys are three weeks late on that project!!" Do you try to pass the buck? "Actually, sir, we got the plans over to McCormick's department to bid the job weeks ago." Do you feign ignorance? "Really? I had no idea. I'll get right on it." Maybe you just weasel your way out of it: "That job's a slam dunk, sir . . .

we'll have it done this week." Years ago I did a tour of duty in the corporate world; the head man was a pretty intimidating guy. Many heads rolled in his office. My plan was basically to try to avoid him at all costs; when I did run into him in the hallway, even in "friendly" conversation, I always felt about ten years old.

How about sports? A few years ago I volunteered to coach for my son's baseball team. There was a mandatory meeting that all coaches needed to attend before the season, to pick up equipment and listen to a "briefing." Our recreation department brought in a retired professional pitcher, a local boy, to give us all a pep talk. The posing that went on was incredible. Here's a bunch of balding dads with beer bellies sort of swaggering around, talking about their own baseball days, throwing out comments about pro players like they knew them personally, and spitting (I kid you not). Their "attitude" (that's a tame word) was so thick I needed waders. It was the biggest bunch of posers I've ever met . . . outside of church.

That same sort of thing goes on Sunday mornings, it's just a different set of rules. Dave runs into Bob in the church lobby. Both are wearing their happy faces, though neither is happy at all. "Hey, Bob, how are ya?" Bob is actually furious at his wife and ready to leave her, but he says, "Great, just great, Dave. The Lord is good!" Dave, on the other hand, hasn't believed in the goodness of God for years, ever since his daughter was killed. "Yep — God is good, all the time. I'm just so glad to be here, praising the Lord." "Me too. Well, I'll be praying for you!" I would love to see a tally of the number of prayers actually *prayed* against the number of prayers promised. I bet it's about one in a thousand. "And I'll be praying for you too. Well, gotta go! You take care." "Take care" is our way of saying, "I'm done with this conversation and I want to get out of here but I don't want to appear rude so I'll say something that sounds meaningful and caring," but in truth, Dave doesn't give a rip about Bob.

STRENGTH GONE BAD

Adam falls, and all his sons with him. After that, what do you see as the story unfolds? Violent men, or passive men. Strength gone bad. Cain kills Abel; Lamech threatens to kill everybody else. God finally floods the earth because of the violence of men, but it's still going on. Sometimes it gets physical; most of the time, it's verbal. I know Christian men who say the most awful things to their wives. Or they kill them with their silence; a cold, deadly silence. I know pastors, warm and friendly guys in the pulpit, who from the safety of their office send out blistering E-mails to their staff. It's cowardice, all of it. I was intrigued to read in the journals of civil war commanders how the men you thought would be real heroes end up just the opposite. "Roughs that are always ready for street fighting are cowards on the open battlefield," declared one corporal. A sergeant from the same division agreed: "I don't know of a single fist-fighting bully but what he makes a cowardly soldier." The violence, no matter what form, is a cover-up for *fear*.

What about the achievers, the men running hard at life, pressing their way ahead? Most of it is fear-based as well. Not all of it, but most of it. For years, I was a driven, type A, hard-charging perfectionist. I demanded a lot of myself and of those who worked for me. My wife didn't like to call me at work, for as she said, "You have your work voice on." In other words, your fig leaf is showing. All that swaggering and supposed confidence and hard charging came out of fear — the fear that if I did not, I would be revealed to be less than a man. Never let down, never drop your guard, give 150 percent.

Achievers are a socially acceptable form of violent men, overdoing it in one way or another. Their casualties tend to be their marriages, their families, and their health. Until a man faces this honestly, and what's really behind it, he'll do great damage.

Then there's the passive men. Abraham is a good example. He's always hiding behind his wife's skirt when the going gets rough. When he and his household are forced by a famine down to Egypt, he tells Pharaoh that Sarah is his sister so that he won't be killed; he jeopardizes her in order to save his own skin. Pharaoh takes Sarah into his harem, but the whole ruse is exposed when God strikes the Egyptians with diseases. You'd think Abraham would have learned his lesson, but no — he does it again years later when he moves to the Negev. In fact, his son Isaac carries on the tradition, jeopardizing Rebekah in the same way. The sins of the father passed along. Abraham is a good man, a friend of God. But he's also a coward. I know many like him. Men who can't commit to the women they've been dragging along for years. Men who won't stand up to the pastor and tell him what they really think. Pastors and Christian leaders who hide behind the fig leaf of niceness and "spirituality" and never, ever confront a difficult situation. Guys who organize their paper clips. Men who hide behind the newspaper or the television and won't really talk to their wives or children.

I'm like him too — a true son of Abraham. I mentioned that the early years of our life in the theater were good ones — but that's not the full story. I also had an affair . . . with my work. I married my wife without ever resolving or even knowing the deeper questions of my own soul. Suddenly, the day after our wedding, I am faced with the reality that I now have this woman as my constant companion and I have no idea what it really means to love her, nor if I have whatever it is she needs from me. *What if I offer her all I have as a man and it's not enough?* That's a risk I was not willing to take. But I knew I had what it took at the theater, and so slowly I began to spend more and more time there. Late nights, weekends, eventually every waking moment. I was hiding, like Adam, running from the fact that my strength was being called for and I really doubted I had any.

The evidence is clear: Adam and Eve's fall sent a tremor through the human race. A fatal flaw entered the original, and it's been passed on to every son and daughter. Thus every little boy and every little girl comes into the world set up for a loss of heart. Even if he can't quite put it into words, every man is haunted by the question, "Am I really a man? Have I got what it takes . . . when it counts?" What follows is the story we are personally much, much more familiar with.

Chapter Four

THE WOUND

Little Billy's mother was always telling him exactly what he was allowed to do and what he was not allowed to do. All the things he was allowed to do were boring. All the things he was not allowed to do were exciting. One of the things he was NEVER NEVER allowed to do, the most exciting of them all, was to go out through the garden gate all by himself and explore the world beyond.

— ROALD DAHL,
THE MINPINS

In the clearing stands a boxer
And a fighter by his trade
And he carries the reminders
Of every glove that laid him down
and cut him till he cried out
in his anger and his shame
"I am leaving, I am leaving"

But the fighter still remains.
— PAUL SIMON
"The Boxer"
(© 1968 by Paul Simon)

*I believe I was the only one in the entire company
to come all the way through Normandy without
getting wounded.*
— PVT. WILLIAM CRAFT,
314TH INFANTRY REGIMENT

The story of Adam's fall is every man's story. It is simple and straightforward, almost mythic in its brevity and depth. And so every man comes into the world set up for a loss of heart. Then comes the story we are much more aware of — our own story. Where Adam's story seems simple and straightforward, our own seems complex and detailed; many more characters are involved, and the plot is sometimes hard to follow. But the outcome is always the same: a wound in the soul. Every boy, in his journey to become a man, takes an arrow in the center of his heart, in the place of his strength. Because the wound is rarely discussed and even more rarely healed, every man carries a wound. And the wound is nearly always given by his father.

A MAN'S DEEPEST QUESTION

On a warm August afternoon several years ago my boys and I were rock climbing in a place called Garden of the Gods, near our home. The red sandstone spires there look like the dorsal fins of some great beast that has just surfaced from the basement of time. We all love to climb, and our love for it goes beyond the adventure. There's something about facing a wall of rock, accepting its challenge and mastering it that calls you out, tests and affirms what you are made of. Besides, the boys are going to climb everything anyway — the refrigerator, the banister, the neighbor's grape arbor — so we might as well take it outside. And it's an excuse to buy some really cool gear. Anyway, when I climb with the boys we always top-rope, meaning that before the ascent I'll rig protection from the top of the rock down, enabling me to belay from the bottom. That way I can coach them as they go, see their every move, help them through the tough spots. Sam was the first to climb that afternoon, and after he clipped the rope into his harness, he began his attempt.

Things were going well until he hit a bit of an overhang, which even though you're roped in makes you feel exposed and more than a little vulnerable. Sam was unable to get over it and he began to get more and more scared the longer he hung there; tears were soon to follow. So with gentle reassurance I told him to head back down, that we didn't need to climb this rock today, that I knew of another one that might be more fun. "No," he said, "I want to do this." I understood. There comes a time when we simply have to face the challenges in our lives and stop backing down. So I helped him up the overhang with a bit of a boost, and on he went with greater speed and confidence. "Way to go, Sam! You're looking good. That's it . . . now reach up to your right . . . yep, now push off that foothold . . . nice move."

Notice what a crucial part of any male sport this sort of "shop talk" is. It's our way of affirming each other without looking like we're affirming. Men rarely praise each other directly, as women do: "Ted, I absolutely love your shorts. You look terrific today." We praise indirectly, by way of our accomplishments: "Whoa, nice shot, Ted. You've got a wicked swing today." As Sam ascended, I was offering words of advice and exhortation. He came to another challenging spot, but this time sailed right over it. A few more moves and he would be at the top. "Way to go, Sam. You're a *wild man*." He finished the climb, and as he walked down from the back side I began to get Blaine clipped in. Ten or fifteen minutes passed, and the story was forgotten to me. But not Sam. While I was coaching his brother up the rock, Sam sort of sidled up to me and in a quiet voice asked, "Dad . . . did you really think I was a wild man up there?"

Miss that moment and you'll miss a boy's heart forever. It's not a question — it's *the* question, the one every boy and man is longing to ask. Do I have what it takes? Am I powerful? Until a man *knows* he's a man he will forever be trying to prove he is one, while at the same time shrink from anything that might reveal he is not. Most men live their lives haunted by the question, or crippled by the answer they've been given.

WHERE DOES MASCULINITY COME FROM?

In order to understand how a man receives a wound, you must understand the central truth of a boy's journey to manhood: Masculinity is *bestowed*. A boy learns who is he and what he's got from a man, or the company of men. He cannot learn it any other place. He cannot learn it from other boys, and he cannot learn it from the world of women. The plan from the beginning of time was that his father would lay the foundation for a young boy's heart, and pass on to him that essential knowledge and confidence in his strength. Dad would be the first man in his life, and forever the most important man. Above all, he would answer *the question* for his son and give him his name. Throughout the history of man given to us in Scripture, it is the father who gives the blessing and

105

thereby "names" the son.

Adam receives his name from God, and also the power of naming. He names Eve, and I believe it is therefore safe to say he also names their sons. We know Abraham names Isaac, and though Isaac's sons Jacob and Esau are apparently named by their mother, they desperately crave the *blessing* that can only come from their father's hand. Jacob gets the blessing, and nearly a century later, leaning on his staff, he passes it on to his sons — he gives them a name and an identity. "You are a lion's cub, O Judah . . . Issachar is a rawboned donkey . . . Dan will be a serpent . . . Gad will be attacked by a band of raiders, but he will attack them at their heels . . . Joseph is a fruitful vine . . . his bow remained steady" (Gen. 49:9, 14, 17, 19, 22, 24). The Baptist's father names him John, even though the rest of the family was going to name him after his father, Zechariah. Even Jesus needed to hear those words of affirmation from his Father. After he is baptized in the Jordan, before the brutal attack on his identity in the wilderness, his Father speaks: "You are my Son, whom I love; with you I am well pleased" (Luke 3:22). In other words, "Jesus, I am deeply proud of you; you have what it takes."

One father-naming story in particular intrigues me. It centers around Benjamin, the last son born to Jacob. Rachel gives birth to the boy, but she will die as a result. With her last breath she names him Ben-Oni, which means "son of my sorrow." But Jacob intervenes and names him Benjamin — "son of my right hand" (Gen. 35:18). This is the critical move, when a boy draws his identity no longer from the mother, but from the father. Notice that it took an active *intervention* by the man; it always does.

MOTHERS AND SONS

A boy is brought into the world by his mother, and she is the center of his universe in those first tender months and years. She suckles him, nurtures him, protects him; she sings to him, reads to him, watches over him, as the old saying goes, "like a mother hen." She often names him as well, tender names like "my little lamb," or "Mama's little sweetheart," or even "my little boyfriend." But a boy cannot grow to manhood with a name like that, let alone a name like "son of my sorrow," and there comes a time for the shift when he begins to seek out his father's affection and attention. He wants to play catch with Dad, and wrestle with him, spend time outside together, or in his workshop. If

107

Dad works outside the home, as most do, then his return in the evening becomes the biggest event of the boy's day. Stasi can tell you when it happened for each of our boys. This is a very hard time in a mother's life, when the father replaces her as the sun of the boy's universe. It is part of Eve's sorrow, this letting go, this being replaced.

Few mothers do it willingly; very few do it well. Many women ask their sons to fill a void in their soul that their husband has left. But the boy has a question that needs an answer, and he cannot get the answer from his mother. Femininity can never bestow masculinity. My mother would often call me "sweetheart," but my father called me "tiger." Which direction do you think a boy would want to head? He will still turn to his mother for comfort (who does he run to when he skins his knee?), but he turns to Dad for adventure, for the chance to test his strength, and most of all, to get the answer to his question. A classic example of these dueling roles took place the other night. We were driving down the road and the boys were talking about the kind of car they want to get when it comes time for their first set of wheels. "I was thinking about a Humvee, or a motorcycle, maybe even a tank. What do you think, Dad?" "I'd go with the Humvee.

We could mount a machine gun on top." "What about you, Mom — what kind of car do you want me to have?" You know what she said . . . "A safe one."

Stasi is a wonderful mother; she has bitten her tongue so many times I wonder that she still has one, as she holds her peace while the boys and I rush off to some adventure begging destruction or bloodshed. Her first reaction — "a safe one" — is so natural, so understandable. After all, she is the incarnation of God's tenderness. But if a mother will not allow her son to become dangerous, if she does not let the father take him away, she will emasculate him. I just read a story of a mother, divorced from her husband, who was furious that he wanted to take the boy hunting. She tried to get a restraining order to prevent him from teaching the boy about guns. That is emasculation. "My mom wouldn't let me play with GI Joe," a young man told me. Another said, "We lived back east, near an amusement park. It had a roller coaster — the old wooden kind. But my mom would never let me go." That is emasculation, and the boy needs to be rescued from it by the active intervention of the father, or another man.

This kind of intervention is powerfully

109

portrayed in the movie *A Perfect World.* Kevin Costner plays an escaped convict who takes a young boy hostage and heads for the state line. But as the story unfolds, we see that what looks like the boy's ruin is actually his *redemption.* The boy is in his underpants when Costner abducts him. That is where many mothers want to keep their sons, albeit unconsciously. She wants her little lamb close by. Over the days that follow, days "together on the road" I might add, Costner and the boy — who has no father — grow close. When he learns that the boy's mother has never allowed him to ride a roller coaster, Costner is outraged. The next scene is the boy, arms high in the air, rolling up and down country roads on the roof of the station wagon. That's the invitation into a man's world, a world involving danger. Implicit in the invitation is the *affirmation,* "You can handle it; you belong here."

There comes a moment when Costner buys the boy a pair of pants (the symbolism in the film is amazing), but the boy won't change in front of him. He is a shy, timid boy who has yet to even smile in the story. Costner senses something is up.

"What's the matter — you don't want

me to see your pecker?"
"It's . . . puny."
"What?"
"It's puny."
"Who told you that?"

The boy, Phillip, is silent. It is the silence of emasculation and shame. The absence of the father's voice is loud and clear. So Costner intervenes, and speaks. "Lemme see . . . go on, I'll shoot you straight." The boy reluctantly bares himself. "No, Phillip. That's a good size for a boy your age." A smile breaks out on his face, like the sun coming up, and you know a major threshold has been crossed for him.

FROM STRENGTH TO STRENGTH

Masculinity is an *essence* that is hard to articulate but that a boy naturally craves as he craves food and water. It is something passed between men. "The traditional way of raising sons," notes Robert Bly, "which lasted for thousands and thousands of years, amounted to fathers and sons living in close — murderously close — proximity, while the father taught the son a trade: perhaps farming or carpentry or blacksmithing or tailoring." My father taught me to fish. We would spend long days together, out in a boat on a lake, trying to catch fish. I will never, ever forget his delight in me when I'd hook one. But the fish were never really the important thing. It was the delight, the contact, the masculine presence gladly bestowing itself on me. "Atta boy, Tiger! Bring him in! That's it . . . well done!" Listen to men when they talk warmly of their fathers and you'll hear the same. "My father taught me to fix tractors . . . to throw a curveball . . . to hunt quail." And despite the details, what is mostly passed along is the masculine blessing.

"Fathers and sons in most tribal cultures live in an amused tolerance of each other," says Bly. "The son has a lot to learn, and so the father and son spend hours trying and failing together to make arrowheads or to repair a spear or track a clever animal. When a father and son spend long hours together, which some fathers and sons still do, we could say that a substance almost like food passes from the older body to the younger." This is why my boys love to wrestle with me — why any healthy boy wants the same with his father. They love the physical contact, to brush against my cheek, feel the sandpaper of my whiskers, my strength all around them, and to test theirs on me.

And it's that *testing* that is so essential. As they've gotten older, they love to start punching matches with me. Luke just did it this morning. I'm downstairs fixing breakfast; Luke senses the opportunity, and he sneaks downstairs and silently stalks me; when he's in range, he lets loose a wallop. It hurts, and *they need to see* that it hurts. Do they have a strength like Dad's? Is it growing, real, substantive? I'll never forget the day when Sam gave me a bloody lip, quite by accident, when we were wrestling. At first he drew back in fear, waiting, I'm sorry to admit, for my anger. Thankfully, on this occasion I just wiped the blood away, smiled, and said, "Whoa . . . nice shot." He beamed; no, he *strutted*. Shook his antlers at me. Word quickly spread through the house and his younger brothers were on the scene, eyes wide at the fact that one of them had drawn blood. New possibilities opened up. Maybe young bucks can take on the old bull.

"The ancient societies believed that a boy becomes a man only through ritual and effort — only through the 'active intervention of the older men,' " Bly reminds us. The father or another man must actively intervene, and the mother must let go. Bly tells the story of one tribal ritual, which involves as they all do the men taking the boy away for initiation. But in this case, when he returns, the boy's mother pretends not to know him. She asks to be introduced to "the young man." That is a beautiful picture of how a mother can cooperate in her son's passage to the father's world. If she does not, things get very messy later — especially in marriage. The boy develops a bond with his mother that is like emotional incest. His loyalties are divided. That is why Scripture says, "For this reason *a man will leave* his father and mother and be united to his wife" (Gen. 2:24, emphasis added).

Sometimes, when the mother clings, the boy will try to tear himself away, violently. This typically comes in the teenage years and often involves some ugly behavior, maybe some foul words on the part of the young man. She feels rejected, and he feels guilty, but he knows he *must* get away. This was my story, and my relationship with my mother has never been good since. I've found that many, many adult men resent their mothers but cannot say why. They simply know they do not want to be close to them; they rarely call. As my friend Dave confessed, "I hate calling my mom. She always says something like, 'It's so good to hear your little voice.' I'm twenty-five and she still wants to call me her little lamb." Somehow, he senses that proximity to his mother endangers his masculine journey, as though he might be sucked back in. It is an irrational fear, but it reveals that both essential ingredients in his passage were missing: Mom did not let go, and Dad did not take him away.

Whatever the mother's failure, it can be overcome by the father's engagement. Let's come back to the rock climbing story with Sam. "Did you really think I was a wild man up there?" He did not ask, "Do you think I am a nice boy?" He asked about his strength, his dangerous capacity to really come through. A boy's passage into manhood involves many of those moments. The father's role is to arrange for them, invite his boy into them, keep his eye out for the moment the question arises and then speak into his son's heart *yes, you are*. You have what it takes. And that is why the deepest wound is always given by the father. As Buechner says, "If strangers and strange sights can shake the world of children, it takes the people they know and love best to pull it out from under them like a chair."

THE FATHER-WOUND

Dave remembers the day the wound came. His parents were having an argument in the kitchen, and his father was verbally abusing his mother. Dave took his mom's side, and his father exploded. "I don't remember all that was said, but I do remember his last words: 'You are such a mama's boy,' he yelled at me. Then he walked out." Perhaps if Dave had a strong relationship with his dad most of the time, a wound like this might be lessened, healed later by words of love. But the blow came after years of distance between them. Dave's father was often gone from morning till night with his own business, and so they rarely spent time together. What is more, Dave felt a lingering disappointment from his dad. He wasn't a star athlete, which he knew his dad highly valued. He had a spiritual hunger and often attended church, which his dad did not value. And so those words fell like a final blow, a death sentence.

Leanne Payne says that when the father-son relationship is right, "the quiet tree of masculine strength within the father protects and nurtures the fragile stripling of masculinity within his son." Dave's father took an ax and gave his hardest blow to his young tree. How I wish it were a rare case, but I am deeply sorry to say I've heard countless stories like it. There's a young boy named Charles who loved to play the piano, but his father and brothers were jocks. One day they came back from the gym to find him at the keyboard, and who knows what else had built up years of scorn and contempt in his father's soul, but his son received both barrels: "You are such a faggot." A man my father's age told me of growing up during the depression; times were hard for his family, and his father, an alcoholic rarely employed, hired him out to a nearby farmer. One day while he was in the field he saw his father's car pull up; he hadn't seen him for weeks, and he raced to meet his dad. Before he could get there his father had grabbed the check for his son's wages, and, spying the boy running toward him, he jumped in the car and sped away. The boy was five years old.

In the case of violent fathers, the boy's question is answered in a devastating way. "Do I have what it takes? Am I a man, Papa?" No, you are a mama's boy, an idiot, a faggot, a seagull. Those are defining sentences that shape a man's life. The assault wounds are like a shotgun blast to the chest. This can get unspeakably evil when it involves physical, sexual, or verbal abuse carried on for years. Without some kind of help, many men never recover. One thing about the assault wounds — they are obvious. The passive wounds are not; they are pernicious, like a cancer. Because they are subtle, they often go unrecognized as wounds and therefore are actually more difficult to heal.

My father was in many ways a good man. He introduced me to the West, and taught me to fish and to camp. I still remember the fried egg sandwiches he would make us for dinner. It was his father's ranch that I worked on each summer, and my dad and I saw a lot of the West together as we'd make the long drive from southern California to Oregon, often with fishing detours through Idaho and Montana. But like so many men of his era, my father had never faced the issues of his own wounds, and he fell to drinking when his life began to take a downhill turn. I was about eleven or twelve at the time — a very critical age in the masculine journey, the age when the question really begins to surface. At the very moment when I am desperately wondering what it means to be a man, and do I have what it takes, my father checked out, went silent. He had a workshop out back, attached to the garage, and he would spend his hours out there alone, reading, doing crossword puzzles, and drinking. That is a major wound.

As Bly says, "Not receiving any blessing from your father is an injury . . . Not seeing your father when you are small, never being with him, having a remote father, an absent father, a workaholic father, is an injury." My friend Alex's father died when he was four years old. The sun in his universe set, never to rise again. How is a little boy to understand that? Every afternoon Alex would stand by the front window, waiting for his father to come home. This went on for almost a year. I've had many clients whose fathers simply left and never came back. Stuart's dad did that, just up and left, and his mother, a troubled woman, was unable to raise him. So he was sent to his aunt and uncle. Divorce or abandonment is a wound that lingers because the boy (or girl) believes if they had done things better, Daddy would have stayed.

Some fathers give a wound merely by their silence; they are present, yet absent to their sons. The silence is deafening. I remember as a boy wanting my father to die, and feeling immense guilt for having such a desire. I understand now that I wanted someone to validate the wound. My father was gone, but because he was physically still around, he was not gone. So I lived with a wound no one could see or understand. In the case of silent, passive, or absent fathers, the question goes unanswered. "Do I have what it takes? Am I a man, Daddy?" Their silence is the answer: "I don't know . . . I doubt it . . . you'll have to find out for yourself . . . probably not."

THE WOUND'S EFFECT

Every man carries a wound. I have never met a man without one. No matter how good your life may have seemed to you, you live in a broken world full of broken people. Your mother and father, no matter how wonderful, couldn't have been perfect. She is a daughter of Eve, and he a son of Adam. So there is no crossing through this country without taking a wound. And every wound, whether it's assaultive or passive, delivers with it a *message*. The message feels final and true, absolutely true, because it is delivered with such force. Our reaction to it shapes our personality in very significant ways. From that flows the false self. Most of the men you meet are living out a false self, a pose, which is directly related to his wound. Let me try to make this clear.

The message delivered with my wound (my father disappearing into his own battles) was simply this: *You are on your own, John. There is no one in your corner, no one to show you the way and above all, no one to tell you if you are or are not a man. The core question of your soul has no answer, and can never get one.* What does a boy do with that? First, I became an unruly teen. I got kicked out of school, had a police record. We often misunderstand that behavior as "adolescent rebellion," but those are cries for involvement, for *engagement*. Even after God's dramatic rescue of me at the age of nineteen, when I became a Christian, the wound remained. As my dear friend Brent said, "Becoming a Christian doesn't necessarily fix things. My arrows were still lodged deep and refused to allow some angry wounds inside to heal."

I mentioned earlier that for years I was a very driven man, a perfectionist, a hard-charger, and a fiercely independent man. The world rewards that kind of drivenness; most of the successful men reading this book are driven. But behind me was a string of casualties — people I had hurt, or dismissed — including my own father. There was the near casualty of my marriage and there was certainly the casualty of my own heart. For to live a driven life you have to literally shove your heart down, or drive it with whips. You can never admit need, never admit brokenness. This is the story of the creation of that false self. And if you had asked my wife during the first ten years of our marriage if we had a good relationship, she probably would have said yes. But if you had asked her if something was missing, if she sensed a fatal flaw, she would have immediately been able to tell you: he doesn't need me. That was my vow, you see. *I won't need anyone.* After all, the wound was deep and unhealed, and the message it brought seemed so final: I am on my own.

Another friend, Stan, is a successful attorney and a genuinely good guy. When he was about fifteen, his father committed suicide — stuck a gun in his mouth and pulled the trigger. His family tried to put it all behind them, sweep it under the rug. They never spoke of it again. The message delivered by that gruesome blow was something like this: *Your background is very dark, the masculine in your family cannot even be spoken of, anything wild is violent and evil.* The effect was another sort of vow: "I will never do anything even remotely dangerous, or risky, or wild. I will never be like my dad (how many men live with that vow?). I won't take one step in that direction. I will be the nicest guy you ever met." You know what? He is. Stan's the nicest guy you could meet — gentle, creative, caring, soft-spoken. And now he hates that about himself; he hates the thought that he's a pushover, that he won't take you on, can't say no, can't stand up for himself.

Those are the two basic options. Men either overcompensate for their wound and become driven (violent men), or they shrink back and go passive (retreating men). Often it's an odd mixture of both. Witness the twin messages sported by young college-age men especially: a goatee, which says, "I'm kind of dangerous," and a baseball hat turned backward, which says, "But really I'm a little boy; don't require anything of me." Which is it? Are you strong, or are you weak? Remember Alex, who stood at the door waiting for a daddy who would never return? You wouldn't in a million years have guessed that was his story if you'd known him in college. He was a man's man, an incredible football player. A hard-drinking, hard-living man every guy looked up to. He drove a truck, chewed tobacco, loved the outdoors. He used to eat glass. I'm serious. It was a sort of frat party trick he took on, the ultimate display of dangerous strength.

He'd literally take a bite out of a glass, chew it slowly and swallow it. When he worked as a bouncer for a tough bar, it made a pretty impressive show to get the roughnecks in line. But it was a show — the whole macho-man persona.

Charles, the artistic boy, the piano player whose father called him a "faggot" — what do you think happened there? He never played the piano again after that day. Years later, as a man in his late twenties, he does not know what to do with his life. He has no passion, cannot find a career to love. And so he cannot commit to the woman he loves, cannot marry her because he is so uncertain of himself. But of course — his heart was taken out, way back there in his story. Dave is also in his twenties now, drifting, deeply insecure, and loaded with a great deal of self-hatred. He does not feel like a man and he believes he never will. Like so many, he struggles with confidence around women and around men he sees as real men. Stuart, whose father abandoned him, became a man without emotion. His favorite character as a boy was Spock, the alien in *Star Trek* who lives solely from his mind. Stuart is now a scientist and his wife is immensely lonely.

On and on it goes. The wound comes,

and with it a message. From that place the boy makes a vow, chooses a way of life that gives rise to the false self. At the core of it all is a deep uncertainty. The man doesn't live from a center. So many men feel stuck — either paralyzed and unable to move, or unable to stop moving. Of course, every little girl has her own story too. But I want to save that for a later chapter, and bring it together with how a man fights for a woman's heart. Let me say a few more words about what happens to a man after the wound is given.

Chapter Five

THE BATTLE FOR A MAN'S HEART

Now you're out there God knows where
You're one of the walking wounded.
> — JAN KRIST
> "Walking Wounded"
> by Ian Krist
> and Paul Murphy

To give a man back his heart is the hardest mission on earth.
> — FROM THE MOVIE *MICHAEL*

Nothing worth having comes without some kind of fight.
> — BRUCE COCKBURN
> "Lovers in a Dangerous Time"
> (written in 1982 for *Stealing Fire*)

A few years ago now my middle son, Blaine, made the big transition to first grade. That's a huge step for any child — leaving the comfort and safety of Mom's side, spending all day at school, being among the "big kids." But Blaine's a very outgoing and winsome boy, a born leader, and we knew he'd handle it swimmingly. Every night at the dinner table he regaled us with tales of the day's adventures. It was fun to recall with him the joys of those early school days — a shiny new lunchbox, brand-new yellow No. 2 pencils, a box of Crayolas with a *built-in sharpener,* a new desk, and new friends. We heard all about his new teacher, gym class, what they played at recess, how he was emerging as a leader in all the games. But then one night he was silent. "What's wrong, Tiger?" I asked. He wouldn't say, wouldn't even look up. "What happened?" He didn't want to talk about it. Finally, the story came out — a bully. Some first-grade poser had pushed him down on the playground in front of all his friends. Tears were streaming down his cheeks as he told us the story.

"Blaine, look at me." He raised his tearful eyes slowly, reluctantly. There was shame written all over his face. "I want you to listen very closely to what I am about to say. The next time that bully pushes you down, here is what I want you to do — are you listening, Blaine?" He nodded, his big wet eyes fixed on mine. "I want you to get up . . . and I want you to hit him . . . as hard as you possibly can." A look of embarrassed delight came over Blaine's face. Then he smiled.

THE BATTLE FOR A MAN'S HEART

Good Lord — why did I give him such advice? And why was he delighted with it? Why are some of *you* delighted with it, while others are appalled?

Yes, I know that Jesus told us to turn the other cheek. But we have really misused that verse. You cannot teach a boy to use his strength *by stripping him of it*. Jesus was able to retaliate, believe me. But he chose not to. And yet we suggest that a boy who is mocked, shamed before his fellows, stripped of all power and dignity should stay in that beaten place because Jesus wants him there? You will emasculate him for life. From that point on all will be passive and fearful. He will grow up never knowing how to stand his ground, never knowing if he is a man indeed. Oh yes, he will be courteous, sweet even, deferential, minding all his manners. It may look moral, it may look like turning the other cheek, but it is merely *weakness*. You cannot turn a cheek you do not have. Our churches are full of such men.

At that moment, Blaine's soul was hanging in the balance. Then the fire came back into his eyes and the shame disappeared. But for many, many men their souls still hang in the balance because no one, *no one* has ever invited them to be dangerous, to know their own strength, to discover that they have what it takes. "I feel there is this stormy ocean within me, and I keep trying to make those waters calm and placid," confessed a young friend in his early twenties. "I would love to be dangerous," he said, sighing. "You mean . . . it's possible? I feel like I have to ask permission." Why on earth would a young man have to ask permission to be a man? Because the assault continues long after the wound has been given. I don't mean to create a wrong impression — a man is not wounded once, but many, many times in the course of his life. Nearly every blow ends up falling in the same place: against his strength. Life takes it away, one vertebra at a time, until in the end he has no spine at all.

FINISHING HIM OFF

I read a case a few years ago about a baby boy who suffered a terrible blow during surgery: his penis was "accidentally removed." The event took place back in the '70s, and a decision was made that reflected the widely held belief that "sex roles" are not truly part of our design, but merely shaped by culture and therefore interchangeable. His genitalia were reconstructed in female form, and he was raised as a girl. That story is a parable of our times. It is exactly what we've tried to do to boys, starting from when they are very young. As Christina Hoff Sommers says in her book *The War Against Boys*, "It's a bad time to be a boy in America." Our culture has turned against the masculine essence, aiming to cut it off early. As one example she points to the way in which the shootings at Columbine High School in Littleton, Colorado, are being used against boys in general.

Most of you will remember the tragic story from April 1999. Two boys walked into the school library and began shooting; when it was all over, thirteen victims and their two assailants were dead. Sommers is alarmed about the remarks of William Pollack, director of the Center for Men at McLean Hospital, and so am I. Here is what he said: "The boys in Littleton are the tip of the iceberg. And the iceberg is *all* boys." The idea, widely held in our culture, is that the aggressive nature of boys is inherently bad, and we have to make them into something more like girls. The primary tool for that operation is our public school system. The average schoolteacher faces an incredible challenge: to bring order to a room of boys and girls, and promote learning. The main obstacle to that noble goal is getting the boys to sit still, keep quiet, and pay attention . . . for an entire day. You might as well hold back the tide. That's not the way a boy is wired, and it's not the way a boy learns. Rather than changing the way we do male education, we try to change males.

As Lionel Tiger reports in his book *The Decline of Males*, boys are three to four times more likely than girls to be diagnosed as suffering from attention deficit disorder (ADD). But maybe they're not sick, maybe, as Tiger says, "This may simply mean they enjoy large-muscle movements and assertive actions . . . Boys as a group appear to prefer relatively boisterous and mobile activities to the sedate and physically restricted behavior that school systems reward and to which girls seem to be more inclined."

Tell me about it. This guy ought to come over to our house for dinner. With three boys at the table (and one man, but with a boyish heart), things get pretty wild at times. Chairs, for the most part, are an option. The boys use them more like gymnastic equipment than restraints. Just the other night, I look over to see Blaine balancing across his chair on his stomach, like an acrobat. At the same moment Luke, our youngest, is nowhere to be seen. Or rather, in the place at the table where his head should be, we can only see a pair of socks, pointing straight up. My wife rolls her eyes. But not our school systems. As Tiger says,

At least three to four times as many boys than girls are essentially defined as ill because their preferred patterns of play don't fit easily into the structure of the school. Well-meaning psycho-managers then prescribe tranquilizing drugs for ADD, such as Ritalin . . . The situation is scandalous. The use of drugs so disproportionately among boys betrays the failure of school authorities to understand sex differences . . . The only disease these boys may have is being male.

But it's not just the schools. (Many of

them, by the way, are doing a heroic job.) How about our churches? A young man recently came to me very angry and distraught. He was frustrated at the way his father, a church leader, was coaching him in sports. He's a basketball player and his team had made the city finals. The night of the big game, as he was heading out the door, his father literally stopped him and said, "Now don't go out there and 'kick butt' — that's just not a nice thing to do." I am not making this up. What a ridiculous thing to say to a seventeen-year-old athlete. Go out there and give 'em . . . well, don't give 'em anything. Just be nice. Be the nicest guy the opposing team has ever met. In other words, be *soft*. That is a perfect example of what the church tells men. Someone I read said the church may have a masculine exterior, but its soul has turned feminine.

Emasculation happens in marriage as well. Women are often attracted to the wilder side of a man, but once having caught him they settle down to the task of domesticating him. Ironically, if he gives in he'll resent her for it, and she in turn will wonder where the passion has gone. Most marriages wind up there. A weary and lonely woman asked me the other day, "How do I get my husband to come alive?"

"Invite him to be dangerous," I said. "You mean, I should let him get the motorcycle, right?" "Yep." She shrank back, disappointment on her face. "I know you're right, but I hate the idea. I've made him tame for years."

Think back to that great big lion in that tiny cage. Why would we put a man in a cage? For the same reason we put a lion there. For the same reason we put God there: he's dangerous. To paraphrase Sayers, we've also pared the claws of the Lion *Cub* of Judah. A man is a dangerous thing. Women don't start wars. Violent crimes aren't for the most part committed by women. Our prisons aren't filled with women. Columbine wasn't the work of two young girls. Obviously, something has gone wrong in the masculine soul, and the way we've decided to handle it is to take that dangerous nature away . . . entirely.

"We know that our society produces a plentiful supply of boys," says Robert Bly, "but seems to produce fewer and fewer men." There are two simple reasons: We don't know how to initiate boys into men; and second, *we're not sure we really want to.* We want to socialize them, to be sure, but *away from* all that is fierce, and wild, and passionate. In other words, away from mas-

134

culinity and toward something more feminine. But as Sommers says, we have
forgotten a simple truth: "The energy, com-
petitiveness, and corporal daring of normal,
decent males is responsible for much of
what is right in the world." Sommers reminds us that during the Columbine mas-
sacre, "Seth Houy threw his body over a
terrified girl to shield her from the bullets;
fifteen-year-old Daniel Rohrbough paid with
his life when, at mortal risk to himself, he
held a door open so others could escape."

That strength so essential to men is also
what makes them *heroes*. If a neighborhood
is safe, it's because of the strength of men.
Slavery was stopped by the strength of men,
at a terrible price to them and their families.
The Nazis were stopped by men. Apartheid
wasn't defeated by women. Who gave their
seats up on the lifeboats leaving the *Titanic*,
so that women and children would be
saved? And have we forgotten — it was a
Man who let himself be nailed to Calvary's
cross. This isn't to say women can't be
heroic. I know many heroic women. It's
simply to remind us that God made men the
way they are because we desperately *need*
them to be the way they are. Yes, a man is a
dangerous thing. So is a scalpel. It can
wound or it can save your life. You don't

make it safe by making it dull; you put it in the hands of someone who knows what he's doing.

If you've spent any time around horses, you know a stallion can be a major problem. They're strong, very strong, and they've got a mind of their own. Stallions typically don't like to be bridled, and they can get downright aggressive — especially if there are mares around. A stallion is hard to tame. If you want a safer, quieter animal, there's an easy solution: castrate him. A gelding is much more compliant. You can lead him around by the nose; he'll do what he's told without putting up a fuss. There's only one problem: Geldings don't give life. They can't come through for you the way a stallion can. A stallion is dangerous all right, but if you want the life he offers, you have to have the danger too. They go together.

WHAT'S REALLY GOING ON HERE, ANYWAY?

Let's say it's June 6, 1944, about 0710. You are a soldier in the third wave onto Omaha Beach. Thousands of men have gone before you and now it is your turn. As you jump out of the Higgins boat and wade to the beach, you see the bodies of fallen soldiers everywhere — floating in the water, tossing in the surf, lying on the beach. Moving up the sand you encounter hundreds of wounded men. Some are limping toward the bluffs with you, looking for shelter. Others are barely crawling. Snipers on the cliffs above continue to take them out. Everywhere you look, there are pain and brokenness. The damage is almost overwhelming. When you reach the cliffs, the only point of safety, you find squads of men with no leader. They are shell-shocked, stunned and frightened. Many have lost their weapons; most of them refuse to move. They are paralyzed with fear. Taking all this in, what would you conclude? What would be your assessment of the situation? Whatever else went through your mind, you'd have to admit, *This is one brutal war,* and no one would have disagreed or thought you odd for having said so.

But we do not think so clearly about life and I'm not sure why. Have a look around you — what do you observe? What do you see in the lives of the men that you work with, live by, go to church alongside? Are they full of passionate freedom? Do they fight well? Are their women deeply grateful for how well their men have loved them? Are their children radiant with affirmation? The idea is almost laughable, if it weren't so tragic. Men have been taken out right and left. Scattered across the neighborhood lie the shattered lives of men (and women) who have died at a soul-level from the wounds they've taken. You've heard the expression, "he's a shell of a man?" They have lost heart. Many more are alive, but badly wounded. They are trying to crawl forward, but are having an awful time getting their lives together; they seem to keep taking hits. You know others who are already captives, languishing in prisons of despair, addiction, idleness, or boredom. The place looks like a battlefield, the Omaha Beach of the soul.

And that is precisely what it is. We are now in the late stages of the long and vicious war against the human heart. I know — it sounds overly dramatic. I almost didn't use the term "war" at all, for fear of being dismissed at this point as one more in the group of "Chicken Littles," Christians who run around trying to get everybody worked up over some imaginary fear in order to advance their political or economic or theological cause. But I am not hawking fear at all; I am speaking honestly about the nature of what is unfolding around us . . . *against us*. And until we call the situation what it is, we will not know what to do about it. In fact, this is where many people feel abandoned or betrayed by God. They thought that becoming a Christian would somehow end their troubles, or at least reduce them considerably. No one ever told them they were being moved to the front lines, and they seem genuinely shocked at the fact that they've been shot at.

After the Allies took the beachhead at Normandy, the war wasn't over. In some ways, it had just begun. Stephen Ambrose has given us many unforgettable stories of what followed that famous landing in *Citizen Soldiers*, his record of how the Allies won the war. Many of those stories are almost parables in their meaning. Here is one that followed on the heels of D-Day. It is June 7, 1944:

Brig. Gen. Norman "Dutch" Cota, assistant division commander of the 29th, came on a group of infantry pinned down by some Germans in a farmhouse. He asked the captain in command why his men were making no effort to take the building. "Sir, the Germans are in there, shooting at us," the captain replied. "Well, I'll tell you what, captain," said Cota, unbuckling two grenades from his jacket. "You and your men start shooting at them. I'll take a squad of men and you and your men watch carefully. I'll show you how to take a house with Germans in it." Cota led his squad around a hedge to get as close as possible to the house. Suddenly, he gave a whoop and raced forward, the squad following, yelling like wild men. As they tossed grenades into the windows, Cota and another man kicked in the front door, tossed a couple of grenades inside, waited for the explosions, then dashed into the house. The surviving Germans inside were streaming out the back door, running for their lives. Cota returned to the captain. "You've seen how to take a house," said the general, still out of breath. "Do you understand? Do you know how to do it now?" "Yes, sir."

What can we learn from the parable? Why were those guys pinned down? First, they seemed almost surprised that they were being shot at. "They're shooting at us, sir." Hello? That's what happens in war — you get shot at. Have you forgotten? We were born into a world at war. This scene we're living in is no sitcom; it's bloody battle. Haven't you noticed with what deadly accuracy the wound was given? Those blows you've taken — they were not random accidents at all. They hit dead center. Charles was meant to be a pianist, but he never touched the piano again. I have a gift and calling to speak into the hearts of men and women. But my wound tempted me to be a loner, live far from my heart and from others. Craig's calling is to preach the gospel, like his father and great-grandfather. His wound was an attempt to take that out. He's a seagull, remember? All he can do is "squawk." I failed to mention Reggie earlier. His dad wounded him when he tried to excel in school. "You are so stupid; you'll never make it through college." He wanted to be a doctor, but he never followed his dream.

On and on it goes. The wound is too well aimed and far too consistent to be accidental. It was an attempt to take you out; to cripple or destroy your strength and get you out of the action. The wounds we've taken were leveled against us with stunning accuracy. Hopefully, you're getting the picture. Do you know why there's been such an assault? The Enemy fears you. You are dangerous big-time. If you ever really got your heart back, lived from it with courage, you would be a huge problem to him. You would do a lot of damage . . . on the side of good. Remember how valiant and effective

God has been in the history of the world? You are a stem of that victorious stalk.

Let me come back to the second lesson of the parable from D-Day plus one. The other reason those men were lying there, pinned down, unable to move is because no one had ever shown them how to take a house before. They had been trained, but not for that. Most men have never been initiated into manhood. They have never had anyone show them how to do it, and especially, how to fight for their heart. The failure of so many fathers, the emasculating culture, and the passive church have left men without direction.

That is why I have written this book. I am here to tell you that you *can* get your heart back. But I need to warn you — if you want your heart back, if you want the wound healed and your strength restored and to find your true name, you're going to have to fight for it. Notice your reaction to my words. Does not something in you stir a little, a yearning to live? And doesn't another voice rush in, urging caution, maybe wanting to dismiss me altogether? *He's being melodramatic. What arrogance.* Or, *maybe some guys could, but not me.* Or, *I don't know . . . is this really worth it?* That's part of the battle, right there. See? I'm not making this up.

OUR SEARCH FOR AN ANSWER

First and foremost, we still need to know what we never heard, or heard so badly, from our fathers. We *need to know* who we are and if we have what it takes. What do we do now with that ultimate question? Where do we go to find an answer? In order to help you find the answer to The Question, let me ask you another: What *have* you done with your question? Where have you taken it? You see, a man's core question does not go away. He may try for years to shove it out of his awareness, and just "get on with life." But it does not go away. It is a hunger so essential to our souls that it will compel us to find a resolution. In truth, it drives everything we do.

I spent a few days this fall with a very successful man I'll call Peter. He was hosting me for a conference on the East Coast, and when Peter picked me up at the airport he was driving a new Land Rover with all the bells and whistles. *Nice car,* I thought. *This guy is doing well.* The next day we drove around in his BMW 850CSi. Peter lived in the largest house in town, and had a vacation home in Portugal. None of this wealth was inherited; he worked for every dime. He loved Formula One racing, and fly-fishing for salmon in Nova Scotia. I genuinely liked him. *Now here's a man,* I said to myself. And yet, there was something missing. You'd think a guy like this would be confident, self-assured, centered. And of course, he seemed like that at first. But as we spent time together I found him to be . . . hesitant. He had all the appearances of masculinity, but none of it felt like it was coming from a true center.

After several hours of conversation, he admitted he was coming to a revelation. "I lost my father earlier this year to cancer. But I did not cry when he died. You see, we were never really close." Ah yes, I knew what was coming next. "All these years, knocking myself out to get ahead . . . I wasn't even en-joying myself. What was it for? I see now . . . I was trying to win my father's approval." A long, sad silence. Then Peter said quietly, through tears, "It never worked." Of course not; it never does. No matter how much you make, no matter how far you go in life, that will never heal your wound or tell you who you are. But, oh how many men buy into this one.

After years of trying to succeed in the world's eyes, a friend still clings stubbornly to that idea. Sitting in my office, bleeding from all his wounds, he says to me, "Who's the real stud? The guy making money." You understand that he's not making much, so he can still chase the illusion.

Men take their souls' search for validation in all sorts of directions. Brad is a good man who for so many years now has been searching for a sense of significance through belonging. As he said, "Out of my wounds I figured out how to get life: I'll find a group to belong to, do something incredible that others will want, and I'll be somebody." First it was the right gang of kids in school; then it was the wrestling team; years later, it was the right ministry team. It has been a desperate search, by his own admission. And it hasn't gone well. When things didn't work out earlier this year at the ministry he was serving, he knew he had to leave. "My heart has burst and all the wounds and arrows have come pouring out. I have never felt such pain. The sentences scream at me, 'I do not belong. I am wanted by no one. I am alone.' "

Where does a man go for a sense of validation? To what he owns? To who pays attention to him? How attractive his wife is? Where he gets to eat out? How well he plays sports? The world cheers the vain search on: Make a million, run for office, get a promotion, hit a home run . . . *be* somebody. Can you feel the mockery of it all? The wounded crawl up the beach while the snipers fire away. But the deadliest place a man ever takes his search, the place every man seems to wind up no matter what trail he's followed, is the woman.

TAKING IT TO EVE

Remember the story of my first kiss, that little darling I fell in love with in the seventh grade and how she made my bicycle fly? I fell in love with Debbie the very same year my father checked out of my story, the year I took my deepest wound. The timing was no coincidence. In a young boy's development, there comes a crucial time when the father must intervene. It arrives early in adolescence, somewhere between the ages of eleven and fifteen, depending on the boy. If that intervention does not happen, the boy is set up for disaster; the next window that opens in his soul is sexuality. Debbie made me feel like a million bucks. I couldn't have put words to it at the time; I had no idea what was really going on. But in my heart I felt I had found the answer to my question. A pretty girl thinks I'm the greatest. What more can a guy ask for? If I've found Juliet, then I must be Romeo.

When she broke up with me, it began

what has been a long and sad story of searching for "the woman that will make me feel like a man." I went from girlfriend to girlfriend trying to get an answer. To be the hero to the beauty — that has been my longing, my image of what it means to really, finally be a man. Bly calls it the search for the Golden-haired Woman.

> He sees a woman across the room, knows immediately that it is "She." He drops the relationship he has, pursues her, feels wild excitement, passion, beating heart, obsession. After a few months, everything collapses; she becomes an ordinary woman. He is confused and puzzled. Then he sees once more a radiant face across the room, and the old certainty comes again. (*Iron John*)

Why is pornography the most addictive thing in the universe for men? Certainly there's the fact that a man is visually wired, that pictures and images arouse men much more than they do women. But the deeper reason is because that seductive beauty reaches down inside and touches your desperate hunger for validation as a man you didn't even know you had, touches it like nothing else most men have ever experienced. You must understand — this is deeper than legs and breasts and good sex. It is mythological. Look at the lengths men will go to find the golden-haired woman. They have fought duels over her beauty; they have fought wars. You see, every man remembers Eve. We are haunted by her. And somehow we believe that if we could find her, get her back, then we'd also recover with her our own lost masculinity.

You'll recall the little boy Philip, from the movie *A Perfect World*? Remember what his fear was? That his penis was puny. That's how many men articulate a sense of emasculation. Later in life a man's worst fear is often impotence. If he can't get an erection, then he hasn't got what it takes. But the opposite is also at work. If a man can feel an erection, well then, he feels powerful. He feels strong. I'm telling you, for many men The Question feels hardwired to his penis. If he can feel like the hero sexually, well, then mister, he's the hero. Pornography is so seductive because what is a wounded, famished man to think when there are literally hundreds of beauties willing to give themselves to him? (Of course, it's not just to him, but when he's alone with the photos, it feels like it's just for him.)

It's unbelievable — how many movies center around this lie? Get the beauty, win her, bed her, and you are the man. You're James Bond. You're a stud. Look carefully at the lyrics to Bruce Springsteen's song, *Secret Garden* (from his *Greatest Hits* recording, 1995):

> She'll let you in her house
> If you come knockin' late at night
> She'll let you in her mouth
> If the words you say are right
> If you pay the price
> She'll let you deep inside
> But there's a secret garden she hides.
> She'll lead you down a path
> There'll be tenderness in the air
> She'll let you come just far enough
> So you know she's really there
> She'll look at you and smile
> And her eyes will say
> She's got a secret garden
> Where everything you want
> Where everything you need
> Will always stay
> A million miles away.

It's a deep lie wedded to a deep truth. Eve *is* a garden of delight (Song 4:16). But she's not everything you want, everything you

149

need — not even close. Of course it will stay a million miles away. You can't get there from here because it's not there. *It's not there.* The answer to your question can never, ever be found there. Don't get me wrong. A woman is a captivating thing. More captivating than anything else in all creation. "The naked woman's body is a portion of eternity too great for the eye of man." Femininity can *arouse* masculinity. Boy oh boy can it. My wife flashes me a little breast, a little thigh, and I'm ready for action. All systems alert. She tells me in a soft voice that I'm a man and I'll leap tall buildings for her. But femininity can never *bestow* masculinity. It's like asking a pearl to give you a buffalo. It's like asking a field of wildflowers to give you a '57 Chevy. They are different substances entirely.

When a man takes his question to the woman what happens is either addiction or emasculation. Usually both.

Dave, whose father blew a hole in his chest when he called him "mama's boy," took his question to the woman. Recently he confessed to me that younger women are his obsession. You can see why — they're less of a threat. A younger woman isn't half the challenge. He can feel more like a man there. Dave's embarrassed by his obsession, but it doesn't stop him. A younger woman feels like the answer to his question *and he's got to get an answer.* But he knows his search is impossible. He admitted to me just the other day, "Even if I marry a beautiful woman, I will always know there is an even more beautiful woman out there somewhere. So I'll wonder — could I have won her?"

It's a lie. As Bly says, it's a search without an end. "We are looking at the source of a lot of desperation in certain men here, and a lot of suffering in certain women." How often I have seen this. A friend's brother hit rock bottom a few years back when his girlfriend broke up with him. He was a really successful guy, a high school star athlete who became a promising young attorney. But he was carrying a wound from an alcoholic, workaholic father who never gave him what every boy craves. Like so many of us, he took his heart with its question to the woman. When she dumped him, my friend said, "it blew him out of the water. He went into a major nosedive, started drinking heavily, smoking. He even left the country. His life was shattered."

This is why so many men secretly fear their wives. She sees him as no one else does, sleeps with him, knows what he's made of. If he has given her the power to validate him as a man, then he has also given her the power to *invalidate* him too. That's the deadly catch. A pastor told me that for years he's been trying to please his wife and she keeps giving him an "F" "What if she is not the report card on you?" I suggested. "She sure feels like it . . . and I'm failing." Another man, Richard, became verbally abusive toward his wife in the early years of their marriage. His vision for his life was that he was meant to be Romeo and therefore, she must be Juliet. When she turned out not to be the Golden-haired Woman, he was furious. Because that meant, you see, that he was not the heroic man. I remember seeing a picture of Julia Roberts without costume and makeup; *Oh,* I realized, *she's just an ordinary woman.*

"He was coming to me for his validation," a young woman told me about the man she was dating. Or, had been dating. She was drawn to him at first, and certainly drawn to the way he was taken with her. "That's why I broke up with him." I was amazed at her perceptiveness and her courage. It's very rare to find, especially in younger women. How wonderful it feels at first to be his obsession. To be thought of as a goddess is pretty heady stuff. But eventually, it all

152

turns from romance to immense pressure on her part. "He kept saying, 'I don't know if I have what it takes and you're telling me I don't.' He'll thank me for it some day."

What's fascinating to note is that homosexuals are actually more clear on this point. They know that what is missing in their hearts is *masculine* love. The problem is that they've sexualized it. Joseph Nicolosi says that homosexuality is an attempt to repair the wound by filling it with masculinity, either the masculine love that was missing or the masculine strength many men feel they do not possess. It, too, is a vain search and that is why the overwhelming number of homosexual relationships do not last, why so many gay men move from one man to another and why so many of them suffer from depression and a host of other addictions. What they need can't be found there.

Why have I said all this about our search for validation and the answer to our question? Because we cannot hear the real answer until we see we've got a false one. So long as we chase the illusion, how can we face reality? The hunger is there; it lives in our souls like a famished craving, no matter what we've tried to fill it with. If you take your question to Eve, it will break your heart. I know this now, after many, many hard years. You can't get your answer there. In fact, you can't get your answer from any of the things men chase after to find their sense of self. There is only one source for the answer to your question. And so no matter where you've taken your question, you've got to take it back. You have to walk away. That is the beginning of your journey.

Chapter Six

THE FATHER'S VOICE

No man, for any considerable period of time, can wear one face to himself and another to the multi-tude without finally getting bewildered as to which may be the truth.
— NATHANIEL HAWTHORNE

Esse quam videri
To be, rather than to appear

Who can give a man this, his own name?
— GEORGE MACDONALD

Summers in the eastern Oregon sagebrush are hot, dry, and dusty. When the sun was high the temperature could soar into the 90s, so whenever possible we saved most of the hard labor on the ranch for the early morning or late afternoon and evening, when the cool air drifted up from the river valley below. Sometimes we'd fix irrigation ditches during the heat of the day, which for me was a great excuse to get really wet. I'd tromp along in the ditch, letting the warm muddy water soak my jeans. But most of the time we'd head back to the ranch house for a glass of iced tea. Pop loved his tea sweetened with a healthy dose of sugar, the way they drink it in the South. We'd sit at the kitchen table and have a glass or two and talk about the events of the morning, or a plan he had to sell some cattle at the auction, or how he thought we'd spend the afternoon.

One day late in the summer of my thirteenth year, Pop and I had just come in for our ritual when he stood up and walked over to the window. The kitchen faced south and from there gave a view over a large alfalfa field and then on toward the pastureland. Like most ranchers Pop grew his own hay, to provide feed for cattle and horses he kept over the winter. I joined him at the window and saw that a steer had gotten out of the range and into the alfalfa. I remembered my grandfather telling me that it's dangerous for a cow to stuff itself on fresh alfalfa; it expands in their stomach like rising bread and could rupture one of their four chambers. Pop was clearly irritated, as only a cowboy can be irritated at cattle. I, on the other hand, was excited. This meant adventure.

"Go saddle up Tony and get that steer," he said, sitting back in his chair and kicking his boots up on the one in front of him. His demeanor made it clear that he was not going with me; he was, in fact, not going anywhere. As he poured himself another glass of tea my mind raced through the implications of what he'd said. It meant I first had to go catch Tony, the biggest horse on the ranch. I was scared of Tony, but we both knew he was the best cattle horse. I had to saddle him up by myself and ride out to get that steer. Alone. Having processed this information I realized I had been standing there for who knows how long and it was time I got going. As I walked out the back porch toward the corral I felt two things and felt them strongly: fear . . . and honor.

Most of our life-changing moments are realized as such later. I couldn't have told you why, but I knew I'd crossed a threshold in my life as a young man. Pop believed in

157

me, and whatever he saw that I did not, the fact that he believed made me believe it too. I got the steer that day . . . and a whole lot more.

DESPERATE FOR INITIATION

A man needs to know his name. He needs to know he's got what it takes. And I don't mean "know" in the modernistic, rationalistic sense. I don't mean that the thought has passed through your cerebral cortex and you've given it intellectual assent, the way you know about the Battle of Waterloo or the ozone layer — the way most men "know" God or the truths of Christianity. I mean a deep knowing, the kind of knowing that comes when you have been there, entered in, experienced firsthand in an unforgettable way. The way "Adam knew his wife" and she gave birth to a child. Adam didn't know *about* Eve; he knew her intimately, through flesh-and-blood experience at a very deep level. There's knowledge *about* and knowledge *of*. When it comes to our question, we need the latter.

In the movie *Gladiator*, set in the second century A.D., the hero is a warrior from Spain called Maximus. He is the commander of the Roman armies, a general loved by his men and by the aging emperor

Marcus Aurelius. The emperor's foul son Commodus learns of his father's plan to make Maximus emperor in his place, but before Marcus can pronounce his successor, Commodus strangles his father. He sentences Maximus to immediate execution and his wife and son to crucifixion and burning. Maximus escapes, but too late to save his family. Captured by slave traders, he is sold as a gladiator. That fate is normally a death sentence, but this is Maximus, a valiant fighter. He more than survives; he becomes a champion. Ultimately he is taken to Rome to perform in the Coliseum before the emperor Commodus (who of course believes that Maximus is long dead). After a remarkable display of courage and a stunning upset, the emperor comes down into the arena to meet the valiant gladiator, whose identity remains hidden behind his helmet.

MAXIMUS:	My name is Gladiator. (He turns and walks away.)
COMMODUS:	How dare you show your back to me?! Slave! You will remove your helmet and tell me your name.
MAXIMUS:	(Slowly, very slowly

lifts his helmet and
turns to face his
enemy)
My name is Maximus
Decimus Meridius;
Commander of the
Armies of the North;
General of the Felix
Legions;
loyal servant to the
true emperor, Marcus
Aurelius;
father to a murdered
son;
husband to a mur-
dered wife;
and I will have my
vengeance, in this life
or in the next.

His answer builds like a mighty wave, swelling in size and strength before it crashes on the shore. Where does a man go to learn an answer like that — to learn his true name, a name that can never be taken from him? That deep heart knowledge comes only through a process of *initiation*. You have to know where you've come from; you have to have faced a series of trials that test you; you have to have taken a journey;

and you have to have faced your enemy. But as a young man recently lamented to me, "I've been a Christian since I was five — no one ever showed me what it means to really be a man." He's lost now. He moved across the country to be with his girlfriend, but she's dumped him because he doesn't know who he is and what he's here for. There are countless others like him, a world of such men — a world of uninitiated men.

The church would like to think it is initiating men, but it's not. What does the church bring a man into? What does it call him out to be? Moral. That is pitifully insufficient. Morality is a good thing, but morality is never the point. Paul says the Law is given as a tutor to the child, but not to the son. The son is invited up into something much more. He gets the keys to the car; he gets to go away with the father on some dangerous mission. I'm struck by the poignancy of the scene at the end of the Civil War, just after Appomattox, where General Robert E. Lee has surrendered to General Ulysses S. Grant. For five years Lee has led the Army of Northern Virginia through some of the most terrible trials men have ever known. You would think they'd be glad to have it over. But Lee's men hang upon the reins of his horse and beg him not to go, plead for one more chance to "whip those Yankees." Lee had become their father, had given those men what most of them had never had before — an identity and a place in a larger story.

Every man needs someone like Robert E. Lee, or that brigadier general from the 29th: "You've seen how to take a house. Do you understand? Do you know how to do it now?" "Yes, sir." We need someone like my grandfather, who can teach us how to "saddle up." But Lee is long gone, brigadier generals are rare, and my grandfather has been dead for many years. Where do we go? To whom can we turn? To a most surprising source.

HOW GOD INITIATES A MAN

A number of years ago, at a point in my own journey when I felt more lost than ever, I heard a talk given by Gordon Dalby, who had just written *The Healing of the Masculine Soul.* He raised the idea that despite a man's past and the failures of his own father to initiate him, God could take him on that journey, provide what was missing. A hope rose within me, but I dismissed it with the cynicism I'd learned to use to keep down most things in my soul. Several weeks, perhaps months later, I was downstairs in the early morning to read and pray. As with so many of my "quiet times," I ended up looking out the window toward the east to watch the sun rise. I heard Jesus whisper a question to me: "Will you let me initiate you?" Before my mind ever had a chance to process, dissect, and doubt the whole exchange, my heart leaped up and said *yes*.

"Who can give a man this, his own name?" George MacDonald asks. "God alone. For no one but God sees what the man is." He reflects upon the white stone that Revelation includes among the rewards God will give to those who "overcome." On that white stone there is a new name. It is "new" only in the sense that it is not the name the world gave to us, certainly not the one delivered with the wound. No man will find on that stone "mama's boy" or "fatty" or "seagull." But the new name is really not new at all when you understand that it is your *true* name, the one that belongs to you, "that being whom he had in his thought when he began to make the child, and whom he kept in his thought throughout the long process of creation" and redemption. Psalm 139 makes it clear that we were personally, uniquely planned and created, knit together in our mother's womb by God himself. He had someone in mind and that someone has a name.

That someone has also undergone a terrible assault, and yet God remains committed to the realization of that same someone. The giving of the white stone makes it clear — that is what he is up to. The history of a man's relationship with God is the story of how God calls him out, takes him on a journey and gives him his true name. Most of us have thought it was the story of how God sits on his throne waiting to whack a man broadside when he steps out of line. Not so. He created Adam for adventure, battle and beauty; he created us for a unique place in his story and he is committed to bringing us back to the original design. So God calls Abram out from Ur of the Chaldeas to a land he has never seen, to the frontier, and along the way Abram gets a new name. He becomes Abraham. God takes Jacob off into Mesopotamia somewhere, to learn things he has to learn and cannot learn at his mother's side. When he rides back into town, he has a limp and a new name as well.

Even if your father did his job, he can only take you partway. There comes a time when you have to leave all that is familiar, and go on into the unknown with God. Saul was a guy who really thought he understood the story and very much liked the part he had written for himself. He was the hero of his own little miniseries, "Saul the Avenger." After that little matter on the Damascus road he becomes *Paul*, and rather than heading back into all of the old and familiar ways he is led out into Arabia for three years to learn directly from God. Jesus shows us that initiation can happen even when we've lost our father or grandfather. He's the carpenter's son, which means Joseph was able to help him in the early days of his journey. But when we meet the young man Jesus, Joseph is out of the picture. Jesus has a new teacher — his true Father — and it is from him he must learn who he really is and what he's really made of.

Initiation involves a journey and a series of tests, through which we discover our real name and our true place in the story. Robert Ruark's book *The Old Man and the Boy* is a classic example of this kind of relationship. There's a boy who needs a lot of teaching, and there's an old man who's got a lot of wisdom. But the initiation doesn't take place at a school desk; it takes place *in the field*, where simple lessons about the land and animals and seasons turn into larger lessons about life and self and God. Through each test comes a *revelation*. The boy must keep his eyes open and ask the right questions. Learning to hunt quail helps you learn about yourself: "He's smart as a whip, and every time you go up against him you're proving something about yourself."

Most of us have been misinterpreting life and what God is doing for a long time. "I think I'm just trying to get God to make my life work easier," a client of mine confessed, but he could have been speaking for most of us. We're asking the wrong questions. Most of us are asking, "God, why did you let this happen to me?" Or, "God, why won't you just . . ." (fill in the blank — help me succeed, get my kids to straighten out, fix my marriage — you know what you've been whining about). But to enter into a journey of initiation with God requires a new set of questions: What are you trying to teach me here? What issues in my heart are you trying to raise through this? What is it you want me to see? What are you asking me to let go of? In truth, God has been trying to initiate you for a long time. What is in the way is how you've mishandled your wound and the life you've constructed as a result.

CONTEMPT FOR THE WOUND

"Men are taught over and over when they are boys that a wound that hurts is shameful," notes Bly. "A wound that stops you from continuing to play is a girlish wound. He who is truly a man keeps walking, dragging his guts behind." Like a man who's broken his leg in a marathon, he finishes the race even if he has to crawl and he doesn't say a word about it. That sort of misunderstanding is why for most of us, our wound is an immense source of shame. A man's not supposed to get hurt; he's certainly not supposed to let it really matter. We've seen too many movies where the good guy takes an arrow, just breaks it off, and keeps on fighting; or maybe he gets shot but is still able to leap across a canyon and get the bad guys. And so most men minimize their wound. "It's not a big deal. Lots of people get hurt when they're young. I'm okay." King David (a guy who's hardly a pushover) doesn't act like that at all. "I am poor and needy," he confesses openly, "and my heart is wounded within me" (Ps. 109:22).

Or perhaps they'll admit it happened, but deny it was a wound because they deserved it. After many months of counseling together about his wound, his vow, and how it was impossible to get The Answer from women, I asked Dave a simple question: "What would it take to convince you that you are a man?" "Nothing," he said. "Nothing can convince me." We sat in silence as tears ran down my cheeks. "You've embraced the wound, haven't you, Dave? You've owned its message as final. You think your father was right about you." "Yes," he said, without any sign of emotion at all. I went home and wept — for Dave, and for so many other men I know and for myself because I realized that I, too, had embraced my wound and ever since just tried to get on with life. Suck it up, as the saying goes. The only thing more tragic than the tragedy that happens to us is the way we handle it.

God is fiercely committed to you, to the restoration and release of your masculine heart. But a wound that goes unacknowledged and unwept is a wound that cannot heal. A wound you've embraced is a wound that cannot heal. A wound you think you deserved is a wound that cannot heal. That is why Brennan Manning says, "The spiritual life begins with the acceptance of our wounded self." Really? How can that be? The reason is simple: "Whatever is denied cannot be healed." But that's the problem, you see. Most men deny their wound — deny that it happened, deny that it hurt, certainly deny that it's shaping the way they live today. And so God's initiation of a man must take a very cunning course; a course that feels very odd, even cruel.

He will wound us in the very place where we have been wounded.

THWARTING THE FALSE SELF

From the place of our woundedness we construct a false self. We find a few gifts that work for us, and we try to live off them. Stuart found he was good at math and science. He shut down his heart and spent all his energies perfecting his "Spock" persona. There, in the academy, he was safe; he was also recognized and rewarded. Alex was good at sports and the whole macho image; he became a glass-eating animal. Stan became the nicest guy you could ever meet. "In the story of my life," he admitted, "I want to be seen as the Nice Guy." I became a hard-charging perfectionist; there, in my perfection, I found safety and recognition. "When I was eight," confesses Brennan Manning, "the impostor, or false self, was born as a defense against pain. The impostor within whispered, 'Brennan, don't ever be your real self anymore because nobody likes you as you are. Invent a new self that everybody will admire and nobody will know.' " Notice the key phrase: "as a defense against pain," as a way of saving himself. The impostor is our plan for salvation.

So God must take it all away. This often happens at the start of our initiation journey. He thwarts our plan for salvation; he shatters the false self. In the last chapter I told you of Brad's plan for self-redemption: he would belong to the "inside group." Even after it failed him time and again, breaking his heart over and over, he wouldn't give it up. He simply thought his aim was off; if he found the *right* group, then his plan would work. Our plan for redemption is hard to let go of; it clings to our hearts like an octopus. So what did God do for Brad? He took it all away. God brought Brad to the point where he thought he had found *the* group, and then God prevented him from maneuvering his way in. Brad wrote me a letter to describe what he was going through:

God has taken all that away, stripped me of all the things I used to earn people's admiration. I knew what he was up to. He put me in a place where my heart's deepest wounds and arrows — and sin

170

— came out. As I was weeping all these pictures of what I want to belong to came up — speaker, counselor, in a group — and it was as if Jesus asked me to give them up. What came from my heart was surprising — incredible *fear*. And then the image of never getting them. A sentence arose in my heart: "You want me to die! If I give those up then I'll never belong and be somebody. You are asking me to die." It has been my hope of salvation.

Why would God do something so cruel? Why would he do something so terrible as to wound us in the place of our deepest wound? Jesus warned us that "whoever wants to save his life will lose it" (Luke 9:24). Christ is not using the word *bios* here; he's not talking about our physical life. The passage is not about trying to save your skin by ducking martyrdom or something like that. The word Christ uses for "life" is the word *psyche* — the word for our soul, our inner self, our heart. He says that the things we do to save our psyche, our self, those plans to save and protect our inner life — those are the things that will actually destroy us. "There is a way that seems right to a man but in the end it leads to death" says

Proverbs 16:25. The false self, our plan for redemption, seems so right to us. It shields us from pain and secures us a little love and admiration. But the false self is a lie; the whole plan is built on pretense. It's a deadly trap. God loves us too much to leave us there. So he thwarts us, in many, many different ways.

In order to take a man into his wound, so that he can heal it and begin the release of the true self, God will thwart the false self. He will take away all that you've leaned upon to bring you life. In the movie *The Natural*, Robert Redford is a baseball player named Roy Hobbs, perhaps the most gifted baseball player ever. He's a high school wonder boy, a natural who gets a shot at the big leagues. But his dreams of a professional career are cut short when Hobbs is wrongly sentenced to prison for murder. Years later, an aging Hobbs gets a second chance. He's signed by the New York Knights — the worst team in the league. But through his incredible gift, untarnished by the years, Hobbs leads the Knights from ignominy to the play-off game for the National League pennant. He rallies the team, becomes the center of their hopes and dreams.

The climax of the film is the game for the championship. It's the bottom of the ninth;

the score is Pittsburgh 2, Knights 0. The Knights have 2 outs; there's a man on first and third when Hobbs steps up to the plate. He's their only chance; this is his moment. Now, there's something you must know, something absolutely crucial to the story. Ever since his high school days, Hobbs has played with a bat he made himself from the heart of a tree felled by lightning in his front yard. Burned into the bat is a lightning bolt and the words "wonder boy." That bat is the symbol of his greatness, his giftedness. He has never, ever played with another. Clutching "wonder boy," Hobbs steps to the plate. His first swing is a miss; his second is a foul ball high and behind. His third is a solid hit along the first-base line; it looks like it's a home run, but it also lands foul. As Hobbs returns to the plate, he sees his bat lying there . . . in pieces. It shattered on that last swing.

This is the critical moment in a man's life, when all he has counted on comes crashing down, when his golden bat breaks into pieces. His investments fail; his company lets him go; the church fires him; he is leveled by an illness; his wife walks out; his daughter turns up pregnant. What is he to do? Will he stay in the game? Will he shrink back to the dugout? Will he scramble to try to put things back together, as so many men do? The true test of a man, the beginning of his redemption, actually starts when he can no longer rely on what he's used all his life. *The real journey begins when the false self fails.* A moment that seems like an eternity passes as Hobbs stands there, holding the broken pieces, surveying the damage. The bat is beyond repair. Then he says to the bat boy, "Go pick me out a winner, Bobby." He stays in the game and hits a home run to win the series.

God will take away our "bat" as well. He will do something to thwart the false self. Stuart "saved" himself by becoming emotionless. Last year his wife walked out on him. She's had it with his two-dimensional existence; what woman wants to be married to Spock? Alex recently suffered a series of panic attacks that left him almost unable to leave his home. The whole macho construct fell to the ground. At first, nobody could believe it; Alex couldn't believe it. He was invincible, the strongest guy you ever met. But it was all built as a defense against the wound. Our loss doesn't necessarily have to be something so dramatic. A man may simply awaken one day to find himself lost, lost as Dante described himself: "In the middle of the road of my life, I awoke in a dark wood, where the true way was wholly lost." That was the turning point in my life.

I went to Washington, D.C., as a young man to try to make something of myself, to prove something, establish credibility. The damnable thing about it was, I succeeded. My giftedness worked against me by coming through for me. I was recognized and rewarded. But the whole experience felt like an act of survival — not something flowing out of a deep center, but something I had to prove, overcome, grasp. As Manning said of his own impostor, "I studied hard, scored excellent grades, won a scholarship in high school, and was stalked every waking moment by the terror of abandonment and the sense that nobody was there for me." At the end of two years I woke one morning and realized I hated my life.

> How many helps thou giv'st to those
> who would learn!
> To some sore pain, to others a sinking
> heart;
> To some a weariness worse than any
> smart;
> To some a haunting, fearing, blind
> concern;
> Madness to some; to some the
> shaking dart

Of hideous death still following as
    they turn;
To some a hunger that will not
    depart.

To some thou giv'st a deep unrest —
    a scorn
Of all they are or see upon the earth;
A gaze, at dusky night and clearing
    morn.
As on a land of emptiness and dearth;
To some a bitter sorrow; to some the
    sting
Of love misprized — of sick aban-
    doning;
To some a frozen heart, oh, worse
    than anything!

The messengers of Satan think to mar,
But make — driving the soul from
    false to real —
To thee, the reconciler, the one real,
In whom alone the *would be* and the *is*
    are met.
    (George MacDonald, *Diary of an
    Old Soul*)

This is a very dangerous moment, when
God seems set against everything that has
meant life to us. Satan spies his opportunity,

and leaps to accuse God in our hearts. *You see,* he says, *God is angry with you. He's disappointed in you. If he loved you he would make things smoother. He's not out for your best, you know.* The Enemy always tempts us back toward control, to recover and rebuild the false self. We must remember that it is out of love that God thwarts our impostor. As Hebrews reminds us, it is the son whom God disciplines, therefore do not lose heart (12:5–6).

God thwarts us to save us. We think it will destroy us, but the opposite is true — we must be saved from what really will destroy us. If we would walk with him in our journey of masculine initiation we must walk away from the false self — set it down, give it up willingly. It feels crazy; it feels immensely vulnerable. Brad has stopped looking for the group. Stuart has begun to open up his heart to emotion, to relationship, to all that he buried so long ago. Alex stopped "eating glass," stopped the whole macho thing to face what he had never faced inside. I gave up perfectionism, left Washington, and went looking for my heart. We simply accept the invitation to leave all that we've relied on and venture out with God. We can choose to do it ourselves, or we can wait for God to bring it all down.

If you have no clue as to what your false

self may be, then a starting point would be to ask those you live with and work with, "What is my effect on you? What am I like to live with (or work with)? What *don't* you feel free to bring up with me?" If you never, ever say a word in a meeting because you fear you might say something stupid, well then, it's time to speak up. If all you ever do is dominate a meeting because your sense of worth comes from being in charge, then you need to shut up for a while. If you've run to sports because you feel best about yourself there, then it's probably time to give it a rest and stay home with your family. If you never play any game with other men, then it's time you go down to the gym with the guys and play some hoops. In other words, you face your fears head-on. Drop the fig leaf; come out from hiding. For how long? Longer than you want to; long enough to raise the deeper issues, let the wound surface from beneath it all.

Losing the false self is painful; though it's a mask, it's one we've worn for years and losing it can feel like losing a close friend. Underneath the mask is all the hurt and fear we've been running from, hiding from. To let it come to the surface can shake us like an earthquake. Brad felt as if he was going to die; you may too. Or you may feel like Andy

Gullahorn, who wrote the song "Steel Bars" from *Old Hat* (© 1997 by Andy Gullahorn):

> So this is how it feels at the rock
>   bottom of despair
> When the house I built comes
>   crashing down
> And this is how it feels when I know
>   the man that I say I am
> Is not the man that I am when no
>   one's around

But this is not the end of the road; it's the trailhead. What you are journeying toward is freedom, healing, and authenticity. Listen to the next part of Andy's song:

> This is how it feels to come alive
>   again
> And start fighting back to gain control
> And this is how it feels to let freedom in
> And break the chains that enslave my
>   soul

WALKING AWAY FROM THE WOMAN

As we walk away from the false self, we will feel vulnerable and exposed. We will be sorely tempted to turn to our comforters for some relief, those places that we've found solace and rest. Because so many of us turned to the woman for our sense of masculinity, we must walk away from her as well. *I do not mean you leave your wife.* I mean you stop looking to her to validate you, stop trying to make her come through for you, stop trying to get your answer from her. For some men, this may mean disappointing her. If you've been a passive man, tiptoeing around your wife for years, never doing anything to rock the boat, then it's time to rock it. Stand up to her; get her mad at you. For those of you violent men (including achievers), it means *you stop abusing her.* You release her as the object of your anger because you release her as the one who was supposed to make you a man. Repentance for a driven man means you become *kind.* Both types are still going to the woman. Repentance depends on which way you've approached her.

But I have counseled many young men to break up with the woman they were *dating* because they had made her their life. She was the sun of his universe, around which he orbited. A man needs a much bigger orbit than a woman. He needs a mission, a life purpose, and he needs to know his name. Only then is he fit for a woman, for only then does he have something to invite her into. A friend tells me that in the Masai tribe in Africa, a young man cannot court a woman until he has killed a lion. That's their way of saying, until he has been initiated. I have seen far too many young men commit a kind of emotional promiscuity with a young woman. He will pursue her, not to offer his strength but to drink from her beauty, to be affirmed by her and feel like a man. They will share deep, intimate conversations. But he will not commit; he is *unable* to commit. This is very unfair to the young lady. After a year of this sort of relationship a dear friend said, "I never felt secure in what I meant to him."

When we feel the pull toward the golden-haired woman, we must recognize that something deeper is at play. As Bly says,

What does it mean when a man falls in love with a radiant face across the room? It may mean that he has some soul work to do. His soul is the issue. Instead of pursuing the woman and trying to get her alone . . . he needs to go alone himself, perhaps to a mountain cabin, for three months, write poetry, canoe down a river, and dream. That would save some women a lot of trouble. (*Iron John*)

181

Again, this is not permission to divorce. A man who has married a woman has made her a solemn pledge; he can never heal his wound by delivering another to the one he promised to love. Sometimes she will leave him; that is another story. Too many men run after her, begging her not to go. If she has to go, it is probably because you have some soul work to do. What I am saying is that the masculine journey always takes a man *away* from the woman, in order that he may come back to her with his question answered. A man does not go to a woman to get his strength; he goes to her to *offer* it. You do not need the woman for you to become a great man, and as a great man you do not need the woman. As Augustine said, "Let my soul praise you for all these beauties, but let it not attach itself to them by the trap of love," the trap of addiction because we've taken our soul to her for validation.

But there is an even deeper issue than our question. What else is it we are seeking from the Woman with the Golden Hair? What is that ache we are trying to assuage with her? Mercy, comfort, beauty, ecstasy — in a word, *God*. I'm serious. What we are looking for is God.

There was a time when Adam drank deeply from the source of all Love. He —

182

our first father and archetype — lived in an unbroken communion with the most captivating, beautiful, and intoxicating Source of life in the universe. Adam had God. True, it was not good for man to be alone, and God in his humility gave us Eve, allowed us to need her as well. But something happened at the Fall; something *shifted*. Eve took the place of God in a man's life. Let me explain.

Adam was not deceived by the serpent. Did you know that? Paul makes it clear in 1 Timothy 2:14 — Adam did not fall because he was deceived. His sin was different; in some ways, it was more serious in that he did it with open eyes. We do not know how long it lasted, but there was a moment in Eden when Eve was fallen and Adam was not; she had eaten, but he yet had a choice. I believe something took place in his heart that went like this: I have lost my *ezer kenegdo,* my soul mate, the most vital companion I've known. I do not know what life will be like, but I know I cannot live without her.

Adam chose Eve over God.

If you think I exaggerate, simply look around. Look at all the art, poetry, music, drama devoted to the beautiful woman. Listen to the language men use to describe her. Watch the powerful obsession at work. What else can this be but *worship?* Men come into the world without the God who was our deepest joy, our ecstasy. Aching for we know not what, we meet Eve's daughters and we are history. She is the closest thing we've ever encountered, the pinnacle of creation, the very embodiment of God's beauty and mystery and tenderness and allure. And what goes out to her is not just our longing for Eve, but our longing for God as well. A man without his true love, his life, his God, will find another. What better substitute than Eve's daughters? Nothing else in creation even comes close.

To a young man who had never been without a girlfriend since the eighth grade, I gave the advice that he should break up, call off all dating for one year. From the look on his face you'd have thought I told him to cut off his arm . . . or something worse. Do you see what is at work here? Notice that the struggle with pornography or masturbation is most difficult when you are lonely, or beat up, or longing for comfort in some way. This will become more intense as you get closer to your wound. The longing for the ache to go away, and the pull toward other comforters can seem overwhelming. I've watched it in many men. I know it in myself. But if this is the water you are truly thirsty for, then why do you remain thirsty after you've had a drink? It's the wrong well.

We must reverse Adam's choice; we must choose God over Eve. We must take our ache to him. For only in God will we find the healing of our wound.

Chapter Seven

HEALING THE WOUND

Desperado, why don't you come to your senses
You been out ridin' fences for so long now
O you're a hard one, but I know
That you got your reasons . . .
You better let somebody love you
Before it's too late.

— THE EAGLES
"Desperado"
(© 1973 by Glenn Fry
and Don Henley)

The task of healing is to respect oneself as a crea-
ture, no more and no less.

— WENDELL BERRY

The deepest desire of our hearts is for union with
God. God created us for union with himself: This
is the original purpose of our lives.

— BRENNAN MANNING

I think I've given a wrong impression of my life with my sons. Rock climbing, canoeing, wrestling, our quest for danger and destruction — you might get the impression we're a sort of military academy of the backwoods or one of those militia cults. So let me tell you of my favorite event of the day. It comes late in the evening, at bedtime, after the boys have brushed their teeth and we've said our family prayers. As I'm tucking them in, one of my boys will ask, "Dad, can we snuggle tonight?" Snuggle time is when I'll cuddle up next to them on a bed that's really not big enough for both of us — and that's the point, to get very close — and there in the dark we'll just sort of talk. Usually we start laughing and then we have to whisper because the others will ask us to "keep it down in there." Sometimes it breaks into tickling, other times it's a chance for them to ask some serious questions about life. But whatever happens, what matters most is what's going on beneath all that: intimacy, closeness, connection.

Yes, my boys want me to guide them into adventure, and they love to test their strength against mine. But all of that takes place in the context of an intimate bond of love that is far deeper than words can express. What they want more than anything,

what I love to offer them more than anything, is soul-to-soul oneness. As Tom
Wolfe said,

> The deepest search in life, it seemed to
> me, the thing that in one way or another
> was central to all living was man's search
> to find a father, not merely the father of
> his flesh, not merely the lost father of his
> youth, but the image of a strength and
> wisdom external to his need and supe-
> rior to his hunger, to which the belief and
> power of his own life could be united.
> ("The Story of a Novel")

THE SOURCE OF REAL STRENGTH

Guys are unanimously embarrassed by their
emptiness and woundedness; it is for most of
us a tremendous source of shame, as I've
said. But it need not be. From the very beginning, back before the Fall and the assault,
ours was meant to be a desperately de-
pendent existence. It's like a tree and its
branches, explains Christ. You are the
branches, I am the trunk. From me you draw
your life; that's how it was meant to be. In
fact, he goes on to say, "Apart from me you
can do nothing" (John 15:5). He's not be-
rating us or mocking us or even saying it with

188

a sigh, all the while thinking, *I wish they'd pull it together and stop needing me so much.* Not at all. We are *made* to depend on God; we are made for union with him and nothing about us works right without it. As C. S. Lewis wrote, "A car is made to run on gasoline, and it would not run properly on anything else. Now God designed the human machine to run on himself. He himself is the fuel our spirits were designed to burn, or the food our spirits were designed to feed on. There is no other."

This is where our sin and our culture have come together to keep us in bondage and brokenness, to prevent the healing of our wound. Our sin is that stubborn part inside that wants, above all else, to be independent. There's a part of us fiercely committed to living in a way where we do not have to depend on anyone — especially God. Then culture comes along with figures like John Wayne and James Bond and all those other "real men," and the one thing they have in common is that they are *loners,* they don't need anyone. We come to believe deep in our hearts that needing anyone for anything is a sort of weakness, a handicap. This is why a man never, ever stops to ask for directions. I am notorious for this. I know how to get there; I'll find my own way,

189

thank you very much. Only when I am fully and finally and completely lost will I pull over and get some help, and I'll feel like a wimp for doing it.

Jesus knew nothing of that. The Man who never flinched to take on hypocrites and get in their face, the One who drove "a hundred men wi' a bundle o' cords swung free," the Master of wind and sea, lived in a desperate dependence on his Father. "I assure you, the Son can do nothing by himself. He does only what he sees the Father doing"; "I live by the power of the living Father who sent me"; "The words I say are not my own, but my Father who lives in me does his work through me." This isn't a source of embarrassment to Christ; quite the opposite. He brags about his relationship with his Father. He's happy to tell anyone who will listen, "The Father and I are one" (John 5:19; 6:57; 14:10; 10:30 NLT).

Why is this important? Because so many men I know live with a deep misunderstanding of Christianity. They look at it as a "second chance" to get their act together. They've been forgiven, now they see it as their job to get with the program. They're trying to finish the marathon with a broken leg. But follow this closely now: You'll recall that masculinity is an essence that is passed from father to son. That is a picture, as so many things in life are, of a deeper reality. The *true* essence of strength is passed to us from God *through our union with him.* Notice what a deep and vital part of King David's life this is. Remembering that he is a man's man, a warrior for sure, listen to how he describes his relationship to God in the Psalms:

I love you, O LORD, my strength. (18:1)

But you, O LORD, be not far off;
O my Strength, come quickly to help me.
(22:19)

O my Strength, I watch for you;
you, O God, are my fortress, my
loving God. (59:9)

I dare say that David could take on John Wayne or James Bond any day; yet this true man is unashamed to admit his desperate dependence on God. We know we are meant to embody strength, we know we are not what we were meant to be, and so we feel our brokenness as a source of shame. As we spoke of his wound recently, and how he needed to enter into it for healing, Dave protested. "I don't even want to go there. It all feels so true." Men are typically quite harsh with the broken places within them. Many report feeling as though there is a boy inside, and they despise that about themselves. *Quit being such a baby,* they order themselves. But that is not how God feels. He is furious about what's happened to you. "It would be better to be thrown into the sea with a large millstone tied around the neck than to face the punishment in store for harming one of these little ones" (Luke 17:2 NLT). Think of how you would feel if the wounds you were given, the blows dealt to you, were dealt to a boy you loved — your son, perhaps. Would you shame him for it? Would you feel scorn that he couldn't rise above it all? No. You'd feel compassion. As Gerard Manley Hopkins wrote,

> My own heart let me more have pity on; let
> Me live to my sad self hereafter kind.

In the movie *Good Will Hunting,* there is a beautiful picture of what can happen when a man realizes he has "owned" his wound, and discovers he doesn't have to. Will Hunting (played by Matt Damon) is a brilliant young man, a genius, who works as a janitor at MIT and lives in a rough part of town. No one knows about his gift, because he hides it behind a false self of "tough kid from the wrong side of the tracks." He's a fighter (a violent man). That false self was born out of a father-wound; his original father he does not know, and the man who was his foster father would come home drunk and beat Will mercilessly. After he's arrested for getting into a brawl for the umpteenth time, Will is ordered by the court to see a psychologist, Sean (played by Robin Williams). They form a bond; for the first time in Will's life, an older man cares about him deeply. His initiation has begun. Toward the end of one of their last sessions, Sean and Will are talking about the beatings he endured, now recorded in his case file.

WILL: So, uh . . . you know, what is it, like "Will has an attachment disorder," is it all that stuff? "Fear of abandonment"? Is that why I broke up with Skyler [his girlfriend]?

SEAN: I didn't know you had.

WILL: I did.

SEAN: You wanna talk about it?

WILL: (Staring at the floor) No.

SEAN: Hey, Will . . . I don't know a lot, but you see this (holding his file) . . . This is not your fault.

WILL: (Dismisses him)Yeah, I know that.

SEAN: Look at me, son. It's not your fault.

WILL: I know.

SEAN: It's not your fault.

WILL: (Beginning to grow defensive) I know.

SEAN: No, no, you don't. It's not your fault.

WILL: (Really defensive) I know.

SEAN: It's not your fault.

WILL: (Trying to end the conversation) All right.

SEAN: It's not your fault . . . it's not your fault.

WILL: (Anger) Don't [mess] with me, Sean, not you.

SEAN: It's not your fault . . . it's not your fault . . . it's not your fault.

WILL: (Collapses into his arms, weeping) I'm so sorry. I'm so sorry.

It is no shame that you need healing; it is no shame to look to another for strength; it is no shame that you feel young and afraid inside. It's not your fault.

194

ENTERING THE WOUND

Frederick Buechner's father committed suicide when he was ten. He left a note, to his mother: "I adore and love you, and am no good . . . Give Freddie my watch. Give Jaime my pearl pin. I give you all my love," and then he sat in the garage while the running car filled it with carbon monoxide. It happened on a Saturday morning in the fall. He was to have taken Frederick and his brother to a football game that day. Instead, he took himself forever from their lives. What is a ten-year-old boy to do with such an event?

A child takes life as it comes because he has no other way of taking it. The world had come to an end that Saturday morning, but each time we had moved to another place, I had seen a world come to an end, and there had always been another world to replace it. When somebody you love dies, Mark Twain said, it is like when your house burns down; it isn't for years that you realize the full extent of your loss. For me it was longer than for most, if indeed I have realized it fully even yet, and in the meantime the loss came to get buried so deep in me that after a time I scarcely ever took it out to look at it at all, let alone speak of it. (*The Sacred Journey*)

That is the way we are with our wound, especially men. We bury it deep and never take it out again. But take it out we must, or better, enter into it. I entered my wound through the surprising door of my anger. After we moved to Colorado, about eleven years ago, I found myself snapping at my boys for silly things. A spilled glass of milk would elicit a burst of rage. *Whoa, John,* I thought, *there are things going on inside, you'd better have a look under the hood.* As I explored my anger with the help of my dear friend Brent, I realized I was so furious about feeling all alone in a world that constantly demanded more of me than I felt able to give. Something in me felt young — like a ten-year-old boy in a man's world but without a man's ability to come through. There was much fear beneath the surface; fear that I would fail, fear that I would be found out, and finally, fear that I was ultimately on my own. *Where did all this fear come from?* I wondered. *Why do I feel so alone in the world . . . and so young inside? Why does something in my heart feel orphaned?*

My answer came through several movies. As I've written about in other places, I was blindsided by *A River Runs Through It* because through its beautiful retelling of boys who never really had their father except during their fishing trips, and how in the end they lost even that. I realized I had lost my father, and like Buechner the loss got buried so deep in me that after a time I scarcely ever took it out. I was pierced by *A Perfect World* because I saw there just how much a boy's father means to him and how I longed for that intimacy with a source of strength who loved me and could tell me my name. I so identified with Will Hunting because I, too, was a fighter who saw myself as up against the rest of the world and I had also accepted my wound and never grieved it. I thought it was my fault.

In some ways God had to sneak up on me through those stories because I wasn't willing to just skip happily down the path to my heart's deepest pain. We fight this part of the journey. The whole false self, our "lifestyle," is an elaborate defense against entering our wounded heart. It is a chosen blindness. "Our false self stubbornly blinds each of us to the light and the truth of our own emptiness and hollowness," says Manning. There are readers who even now have no idea what their wound is, or even what false self arose from it. Ah, how convenient that blindness is. Blissful ignorance. But a wound unfelt is a wound unhealed. We must go in. The door may be your anger; it may be rejection that you've experienced, perhaps from a girl; it may be failure, or the loss of the golden bat and the way God is thwarting your false self. It may be a simple prayer: Jesus, take me into my wound.

"Behold," he says, "I stand at the door and knock."

HEALING THE WOUND

If you wanted to learn how to heal the blind and you thought that following Christ around and watching how he did it would make things clear, you'd wind up pretty frustrated. He never does it the same way twice. He spits on one guy; for another, he spits on the ground and makes mud and puts that on his eyes. To a third he simply speaks, a fourth he touches, and a fifth he kicks out a demon. There are no formulas with God. The way in which God heals our wound is a deeply personal process. He is a person and he insists on working personally. For some, it comes in a moment of divine touch. For others, it takes place over time and through the help of another, maybe several others. As Agnes

Sanford says, "There are in many of us wounds so deep that only the mediation of someone else to whom we may 'bare our grief' can heal us."

So much healing took place in my life simply through my friendship with Brent. We were partners, but far more than that, we were friends. We spent hours together fly-fishing, backpacking, hanging out in pubs. Just spending time with a man I truly respected, a real man who loved and respected me — nothing heals quite like that. At first I feared that I was fooling him, that he'd see through it any day and drop me. But he didn't, and what happened instead was validation. My heart knew that if a man I *know* is a man thinks I'm one, too, well then, maybe I am one after all. Remember — masculinity is bestowed by masculinity. But there have been other significant ways in which God has worked — times of healing prayer, times of grieving the wound and forgiving my father. Most of all, times of deep communion with God. The point is this: Healing never happens outside of intimacy with Christ. The healing of our wound flows out of our union with him.

But there are some common themes that I share with you as you seek the restoration of your heart. The first step seems so simple it's almost hard to believe we overlook it, never ask for it, and when we do, we sometimes struggle for days just to get the words out.

It begins with surrender. As Lewis says, "Until you have given yourself to him you will not have a real self." We return the branch to its trunk; we yield our lives to the One who is our Life. And then *we invite Jesus into the wound;* we ask him to come and meet us there, to enter into the broken and unhealed places of our heart. When the Bible tells us that Christ came to "redeem mankind" it offers a whole lot more than forgiveness. To simply forgive a broken man is like telling someone running a marathon, "It's okay that you've broken your leg. I won't hold that against you. Now finish the race." That is cruel, to leave him disabled that way. No, there is much more to our redemption. The core of Christ's mission is foretold in Isaiah 61:

> The Spirit of the Sovereign LORD is
>   on me,
> because the LORD has anointed me
> to preach good news to the poor.
> He has sent me to bind up the bro-
>   kenhearted,
> to proclaim freedom for the captives

and release for the prisoners. (v, 1)

The Messiah will come, he says, to bind up and heal, to release and set free. What? *Your heart.* Christ comes to restore and release you, your soul, the true you. This is *the* central passage in the entire Bible about Jesus, the one he chooses to quote about himself when he steps into the spotlight in Luke 4 and announces his arrival. So take him at his word — ask him in to heal all the broken places within you and unite them into one whole and healed heart. Ask him to release you from all bondage and captivity, as he promised to do. As MacDonald prayed, "Gather my broken fragments to a whole . . . Let mine be a merry, all-receiving heart, but make it a whole, with light in every part." But you can't do this at a distance; you can't ask Christ to come into your wound while you remain far from it. You have to go there with him.

That is why we must grieve the wound. It was not your fault and it did matter. Oh what a milestone day that was for me when I simply allowed myself to say that the loss of my father *mattered.* The tears that flowed were the first I'd ever granted my wound, and they were deeply healing. All those years of sucking it up melted away in my grief. It is so important for us to grieve our wound; it is the only honest thing to do. For in grieving we admit the truth — that we were hurt by someone we loved, that we lost something very dear, and it hurt us very much. Tears are healing. They help to open and cleanse the wound. As Augustine wrote in his *Confessions*, "The tears . . . streamed down, and I let them flow as freely as they would, making of them a pillow for my heart. On them it rested." Grief is a form of validation; it says the wound *mattered*.

We let God love us; we let him get real close to us. I know, it seems painfully obvious, but I'm telling you few men are ever so vulnerable as to simply let themselves be loved by God. After Brad lost his plan for redemption, I asked him, "Brad, why don't you just let God love you?" He squirmed in his chair. "I have such a hard time with that, just being loved. It feels so naked. I'd rather be in control, be admired for what I bring to the group." Later he wrote this in a letter to me:

After it all came crashing down, I was overwhelmed by sadness and grief. The pain is incredible. In the midst of that God asked me, "Brad, will you let me love you?" I know what he is asking. I feel anxious that I need to go e-mail all these schools and secure a future. But I'm tired of running away. I want to come home. I flipped through my Bible and came to John 15, "Just as the Father has loved you, I have also loved you, abide in my love." The battle is very intense. At times it is all clear. At others it is a fog. Right now all I can do is cling to Jesus as best I know how and not run from all that is in my heart.

Abiding in the love of God is our only hope, the only true home for our hearts. It's not that we mentally acknowledge that God loves us. It's that we let our hearts come home to him, and stay in his love. Mac-Donald says it this way:

When our hearts turn to him, that is opening the door to him . . . then he comes in, not by our thought only, not in our idea only, but he comes himself, and of his own will. Thus the Lord, the Spirit, becomes the soul of our souls . . . Then indeed we *are;* then indeed we have life; the life of Jesus has . . . become life in us . . . we are one with God forever and ever. (*The Heart of George Mac-Donald*)

Or as St. John of the Cross echoes, "O how gently and how lovingly dost thou lie awake in the depth and centre of my soul, where thou in secret and in silence alone, as its sole Lord, abidest, not only as in Thine own house or in Thine own chamber, but also as within my own bosom, in close and intimate union" (*Living Flame of Love*). This deep intimate union with Jesus and with his Father is the source of all our healing and all our strength. It is, as Leanne Payne says, "the central and unique truth of Christianity." After a retreat in which I laid out the masculine journey to a small group of men, I received this E-mail:

My father never left, he just never had time for me or words of encouragement. He has spent his entire life making himself the center of attention. For the first time I understand why I am highly driven, why I never let anyone get close to me — including my wife — and why I am an impostor to most people. I broke down and cried. I feel the presence of God in my heart like I have never felt him before . . . the beginning of a new heart.

Time has come for us to forgive our fathers. Paul warns us that unforgiveness and bitterness can wreck our lives and the lives of others (Eph. 4:31; Heb. 12:15). I am sorry to think of all the years my wife endured the anger and bitterness that I redirected at her from my father. As someone has said, forgiveness is setting a prisoner free and then discovering the prisoner was you. I found some help in Bly's experience of forgiving his own father, when he said, "I began to think of him not as someone who had deprived me of love or attention or companionship, but as someone who himself had been deprived, by his father and his mother and by the culture." My father had his own wound that no one ever offered to heal. His father was an alcoholic, too, for a time, and there were some hard years for my dad as a young man just as there were for me.

Now you must understand: Forgiveness is a choice. It is not a feeling, but an act of the will. As Neil Anderson has written, "Don't wait to forgive until you feel like forgiving; you will never get there. Feelings take time to heal after the choice to forgive is made." We allow God to bring the hurt up from our past, for "if your forgiveness doesn't visit the emotional core of your life, it will be incomplete." We acknowledge that it hurt, that it mattered, and we choose to extend

205

forgiveness to our father. This is *not* saying, "It didn't really matter"; it is *not* saying, "I probably deserved part of it anyway." Forgiveness says, "It was wrong, it mattered, and I release you."

And then we ask God to father us, and to tell us our true name.

GOD'S NAME FOR US

I noticed a few years ago, a ways into my own masculine journey, that I related well to Jesus and to "God" but not to God as *Father.* It's not hard to figure out why. Father has been a source of pain and disappointment to me . . . to many of us. Then I read this in Mac-Donald:

> In my own childhood and boyhood my father was the refuge from all the ills of life, even sharp pain itself. Therefore I say to son or daughter who has no pleasure in the name *Father,* "You must interpret the word by all that you have missed in life. All that human tenderness can give or desire in the nearness and readiness of love, all and infinitely more must be true of the perfect Father — of the maker of fatherhood." (*The Heart of George MacDonald*)

The gift was perfectly timed, for I knew it was time to allow God to father me. (All along the process of my initiation, God has provided words like that, messages, people, gifts to open the next leg of the journey.) Masculinity is passed from father to son, and then from Father to son. Adam, Abraham, Jacob, David, Jesus — they all learned who they were out of their intimacy with God, with the Father. After all, who can give a man this, his own name? God alone. For no one but God sees what the man is. This is usually thought of with a sense of guilt — yes, *God sees me . . . and what he sees is my sin.* That's wrong on two counts.

First off, your sin has been dealt with. Your Father has removed it from you "as far as the east is from the west" (Ps. 103:12). Your sins have been washed away (1 Cor. 6:11). When God looks at you he does not see your sin. He has not one condemning thought toward you (Rom. 8:1). But that's not all. You have a new heart. That's the promise of the new covenant: "I will give you a new heart and put a new spirit in you; I will remove from you your heart of stone and give you a heart of flesh. And I will put my Spirit in you and move you to follow my decrees and be careful to keep my laws"

(Ezek. 36:26–27). There's a reason that it's called good news.

Too many Christians today are living back in the old covenant. They've had Jeremiah 17:9 drilled into them and they walk around believing *my heart is deceitfully wicked*. Not anymore it's not. Read the rest of the book. In Jeremiah 31:33, God announces the cure for all that: "I will put my law in their minds and write it on their hearts. I will be their God, and they will be my people." I will give you a new heart. That's why Paul says in Romans 2:29, "No, a man is a Jew if he is one inwardly; and circumcision is circumcision of the heart, by the Spirit." Sin is not the deepest thing about you. You have a new heart. Did you hear me? Your heart is *good.*

What God sees when he sees you is the *real* you, the true you, the man he had in mind when he made you. How else could he give you the white stone with your true name on it? I've brought you along in Dave's story — how his father dealt him the wound of "mama's boy," how he sought his sense of masculinity through women, how he embraced his wound and its message as final and true. We sat together one day in my office, his life pretty well detailed and unpacked before us, as if we had unpacked a trunk of secrets and laid them all out to the light of day. What else was there to say? "You've only got one hope, Dave . . . that your dad was wrong about you."

You must ask God what he thinks of you, and you must stay with the question until you have an answer. The battle will get fierce here. This is the *last* thing the Evil One wants you to know. He will play the ventriloquist; he'll whisper to you as if he were the voice of God. Remember, he's the accuser of the brethren (Rev. 12:10). After I saw *Gladiator*, I so longed to be a man like Maximus. He reminded me of Henry V, from Shakespeare's play — a courageous, valiant man. Maximus is strong and courageous and he fights so well; yet his heart is given over to eternity. He yearns for heaven but stays to fight so that others might be free. I wept at the end, pierced by a longing to be like him. Satan was all over that, telling me that no, I was really Commodus — the conniving wretch who plays the villain in the movie. What made that blow so hard to shake is the fact that I once was Commodus; I was a selfish, conniving man who manipulated everything for my own benefit. That was a long time ago, but the accusation stung.

I left for a trip to England where I did four

conferences in five days. It was a brutal trip and I was under a great deal of spiritual attack. What a relief it was to slump into my seat and catch my plane home. Tired to the bone, spent and beat up, I needed to hear words from my Father. So I began to pour my heart out to him in my journal.

What of me, dear Lord? Are you pleased? What did you see? I am sorry that I have to ask, wishing I knew without asking. Fear, I suppose, makes me doubt. Still, I yearn to hear from you — a word, or image, a name or even just a glance from you.

This is what I heard:

You are Henry V after Agincourt . . . the man in the arena, whose face is covered with blood and sweat and dust, who strove valiantly . . . a great warrior . . . yes, even Maximus.

And then

You are my friend.

I cannot tell you how much those words mean to me. In fact, I'm embarrassed to tell them to you; they seem arrogant. But I share them in hopes that they will help you find your own. They are words of life, words that heal my wound and shatter the Enemy's accusations. I am grateful for them; deeply grateful. Oh, what wonderful stories I could tell here of how many times God has spoken to me and to other men since we've been asking the question. My friend Aaron went to a park near our home and found a place of solitude. There he waited for the Father's voice. What he first heard was this: "True masculinity is spiritual." Aaron has for so long felt that spirituality was feminine; it put him in a terrible bind because he is a very spiritual man, and yet longs to be a real man. God spoke exactly what he needed to hear — masculinity is spiritual. Then he heard, "True spirituality is good." And then, "You are a man. You are a man. You are a man."

It's a battle to get to this place, and once words like these have been spoken the Enemy rushes in to steal them. Remember how he assaulted Christ in the wilderness, right on the heels of hearing words from his Father. Another friend and I were talking about these stories and many more like them. He sort of sighed and said, "Yes, I remember a time in church when I heard God

211

say to me, 'You're doing great. I am proud of you, right where you are.' But I could not believe it. It just doesn't seem true." That is why we always rest on propositional truth. We stand on what Scripture says about us. We are forgiven. Our heart is good. The Father's voice is *never* condemning. From that place we ask God to speak personally to us, to break the power of the lie that was delivered with our wound.

He knows your name.

OUT OF OUR WOUND COMES OUR GLORY

I have a favorite painting in my office, a reprint of Charlie Schreyvogel's *My Bunkie*. It's a scene of four cavalry soldiers done in the Western style of Remington. The action is a rescue; one of the riders has apparently been shot off his horse and three men are galloping in to pick him up. In the foreground, the stranded soldier is being swept up onto the back of the horse of his bunk mate (his "bunkie"), while the other two are providing rifle cover. I love this scene because that is what I want to do and be; I want to ride to the rescue of those who have been shot down. But sitting in my office one day, God began to speak to me about the painting and my role in it. *You cannot be the man who rescues, John, until you are the man without a horse, the man who needs rescuing.*

Yes. True strength does not come out of bravado. Until we are broken, our life will be self-centered, self-reliant; our strength will be our own. So long as you think you are really something in and of yourself, what will you need God for? I don't trust a man who hasn't suffered; I don't let a man get close to me who hasn't faced his wound. Think of the posers you know — are they the kind of man you would call at 2:00 A.M., when life is collapsing around you? Not me. I don't want clichés; I want deep, soulful truth, and that only comes when a man has walked the road I've been talking about. As Buechner says,

To do for yourself the best that you have it in you to do — to grit your teeth and clench your fists in order to survive the world at its harshest and worst — is, by that very act, to be unable to let something be done for you and in you that is more wonderful still. The trouble with steeling yourself against the harshness of reality is that the same steel that secures your life against being destroyed secures your life also against being opened up

213

and transformed. (*The Sacred Journey*)

Only when we enter our wound will we discover our true glory. As Bly says, "Where a man's wound is, that is where his genius will be." There are two reasons for this. First, because the wound was given in the place of your true strength, as an effort to take you out. Until you go there you are still posing, offering something more shallow and insubstantial. And therefore, second, it is out of your brokenness that you discover what you have to offer the community. The false self is never wholly false. Those gifts we've been using are often quite true about us, but we've used them to hide behind. We thought that the power of our life was in the golden bat, but the power is in *us*. When we begin to offer not merely our gifts but our true selves, that is when we become powerful.

That is when we are ready for battle.

Chapter Eight

A BATTLE TO FIGHT: THE ENEMY

Enemy-occupied territory — that is what this world is.

— C. S. LEWIS

We are but warriors for the working-day;
Our gayness and our gilt are all besmirch'd
With rainy marching in the painful field . . .
But, by the mass, our hearts are in the trim.

— HENRY V

If we would endeavor, like men of courage, to stand in the battle, surely we would feel the favorable assistance of God from Heaven. For he who giveth us occasion to fight, to the end we may get the victory, is ready to succor those that fight manfully, and do trust in his grace.

— THOMAS À KEMPIS

215

"Dad, are there any castles anymore?" Luke and I were sitting at the breakfast table; actually, he was seated and I was attending his Royal Highness, making him toast with apricot jam. As soon as he asked the question I knew what his young heart was wondering. Are there any great adventures anymore? Are there any great battles? I wanted to explain that indeed there are, but before I could reply he got this gleam in his eye and asked, "And are there any dragons?" O, how deeply this is written into the masculine soul. The boy is a warrior; the boy is his name. A man needs a battle to fight; he needs a place for the warrior in him to come alive and be honed, trained, seasoned. If Bly is right (and I believe he is), that "the early death of a man's warriors keeps the boy in him from growing up," then the opposite is true — if we can reawaken that fierce quality in a man, hook it up to a higher purpose, release the warrior within, then the boy can grow up and become truly masculine.

As I was working on this book a few days ago, Blaine came downstairs and without a word slipped a drawing he had made in front of me. It is a pencil sketch of an angel with broad shoulders and long hair; his wings are sweeping around him as if just unfurled to reveal that he is holding a large two-handed sword like a Scottish claymore. He holds the blade upright, ready for action; his gaze is steady and fierce. Beneath the drawing are the words, written in the hand of a nine-year-old boy, "Every man is a warrior inside. But the choice to fight is his own." And a little child shall lead them. Blaine knows as deeply as he knows anything that every man is a warrior, yet every man must choose to fight. The warrior is not the only role a man must play; there are others we will explore later. But the warrior is crucial in our movement toward any masculine integrity; it is hardwired into every man.

THE WARRIOR HEART

I have in my files a copy of a letter written by Major Sullivan Ballou, a Union officer in the 2nd Rhode Island. He writes to his wife on the eve of the Battle of Bull Run, a battle he senses will be his last. He speaks tenderly to her of his undying love, of "the memories of blissful moments I have spent with you." Ballou mourns the thought that he must give up "the hope of future years, when, God willing, we might still have lived and loved together, and seen our sons grown up to honorable manhood around us." Yet in spite of

217

his love the battle calls and he cannot turn from it. "I have no misgivings about, or lack of confidence in the cause in which I am engaged, and my courage does not halt or falter . . . how great a debt we owe to those who went before us through the blood and sufferings of the Revolution . . . Sarah, my love for you is deathless, it seems to bind me with mighty cables that nothing but Omnipotence could break" and yet a greater cause "comes over me like a strong wind and bears me unresistably on with all these chains to the battle field."

A man must have a battle to fight, a great mission to his life that involves and yet transcends even home and family. He must have a cause to which he is devoted even unto death, for this is written into the fabric of his being. Listen carefully now: *You do.* That is why God created you — to be his intimate *ally,* to join him in the Great Battle. You have a specific place in the line, a mission God made you for. That is why it is so essential to hear from God about your true name, because in that name is the mission of your life. Churchill was called upon to lead the British through the desperate hours of WWII. He said, "I felt as if I were walking with destiny, and that all my past life had been but a preparation for this hour and for this trial." The same is true of you; your whole life has been preparation.

"I'd love to be William Wallace, leading the charge with a big sword in my hand," sighed a friend. "But I feel like I'm the guy back there in the fourth row, with a hoe." That's a lie of the Enemy — that your place is really insignificant, that you aren't really armed for it anyway. In your life you *are* William Wallace — who else could be? There is no other man who can replace you in your life, in the arena you've been called to. If you leave your place in the line, it will remain empty. No one else can be who you are meant to be. You *are* the hero in your story. Not a bit player, not an extra, but the main man. This is the next leg in the initiation journey, when God calls a man forward to the front lines. He wants to develop and release in us the qualities every warrior needs — including a keen awareness of the enemies we will face.

Above all else, a warrior has a *vision*, he has a transcendence to his life, a cause greater than self-preservation. The root of all our woes and our false self was this: We were seeking to save our life and we lost it. Christ calls a man beyond that, "but whoever loses his life for me and for the gospel will save it" (Mark 8:35). Again, this isn't just about being willing to die for Christ; it's much more daily than that. For years all my daily energy was spent trying to beat the trials in my life and arrange for a little pleasure. My weeks were wasted away either striving or indulging. I was a mercenary. A mercenary fights for pay, for his own benefit; his life is devoted to himself. "The quality of a true warrior," says Bly, "is that he is in service to a purpose greater than himself; that is, to a transcendent cause." That is the moving quality in Ballou's letter; that is the secret of the warrior-heart of Jesus.

Second, a warrior is *cunning*. He knows when to fight and when to run; he can sense a trap and never charges blindly ahead; he knows what weapons to carry and how to use them. Whatever specific terrain you are called to — at home, at work, in the realm of the arts or industry or world politics, you will always encounter three enemies: the world, the flesh, and the devil. They make up a sort of unholy trinity. Because they always conspire together it's a bit difficult to talk about them individually; in any battle at least two of them are involved, but usually it's all three. Still, they each have their own personality, so I'll take them one at a time and then try to show how they collude against us. Let's start with the enemy closest at hand.

THE TRAITOR WITHIN

> However strong a castle may be, if a treacherous party resides inside (ready to betray at the first opportunity possible), the castle cannot be kept safe from the enemy. Traitors occupy our own hearts, ready to side with every temptation and to surrender to them all. (John Owen, *Sin and Temptation*)

Ever since that fateful day when Adam gave away the essence of his strength, men have struggled with a part of themselves that is ready at the drop of a hat to do the same. We don't want to speak up unless we know it will go well, and we don't want to move unless we're guaranteed success. What the Scriptures call the flesh, the old man, or the sinful nature, is that part of fallen Adam in every man that always wants the easiest way out. It's much easier to masturbate than to make love to your wife, especially if things are not well between you and initiating sex with her feels risky. It's much easier to go down to the driving range and attack a bucket of balls than it is to face the people at work who are angry at you. It's much easier to clean the garage, organize your files, cut the grass, or work on the car than it is to talk to your teenage daughter.

To put it bluntly, your flesh is a weasel, a poser, and a selfish pig. And your flesh is *not you*. Did you know that? Your flesh is not the real you. When Paul gives us his famous passage on what it's like to struggle with sin (Rom. 7), he tells a story we are all too familiar with:

> I decide to do good, but I don't *really* do it; I decide not to do bad, but then I do it anyway. My decisions, such as they are, don't result in actions. Something has gone wrong deep within me and gets the better of me every time. It happens so regularly that it's predictable. The moment I decide to do good, sin is there to trip me up. I truly delight in God's commands, but it's pretty obvious that not all of me joins in that delight. Parts of me covertly rebel, and just when I least expect it, they take charge. (*The Message*)

Okay, we've all been there many times. But what Paul concludes is just astounding: "I am not really the one doing it; the sin within me is doing it" (Rom. 7:20 NLT). Did you notice the distinction he makes? Paul says, "Hey, I know I struggle with sin. But I also know that *my sin is not me* — this is not my true heart." You are not your sin; sin is no longer the truest thing about the man who has come into union with Jesus. Your heart is good. "I will give you a new heart and put a new spirit in you . . ." (Ezek. 36:26). The Big Lie in the church today is that you are nothing more than "a sinner saved by grace." You are a lot more than that. You are a new creation in Christ. The New Testament calls you a saint, a holy one, a son of God. In the core of your being you are a good man. Yes, there is a war within us, but it is a *civil* war. The battle is not between us and God; no, there is a traitor within who wars against our true heart fighting alongside the Spirit of God in us:

> A new power is in operation. The Spirit of life in Christ, like a strong wind, has magnificently cleared the air, freeing you from a fated lifetime of brutal tyranny at the hands of sin and death . . . Anyone, of course, who has not welcomed this invisible but clearly present God, the Spirit of Christ, won't know what we're talking about. But for you who welcome him, in whom he dwells . . . if the alive-and-

present God who raised Jesus from the dead moves into your life, he'll do the same thing in you that he did in Jesus . . . When God lives and breathes in you (and he does, as surely as he did in Jesus), you are delivered from that dead life. (Rom. 8:2–3, 9–11 *The Message*)

The *real* you is on the side of God against the false self. Knowing this makes all the difference in the world. The man who wants to live valiantly will lose heart quickly if he believes that his heart is nothing but sin. Why fight? The battle feels lost before it even begins. No, your flesh is your *false self* — the poser, manifest in cowardice and self-preservation — and the only way to deal with it is to crucify it. Now follow me very closely here: We are never, ever told to crucify our heart. We are never told to kill the true man within us, never told to get rid of those deep desires for battle and adventure and beauty. We are told to shoot the traitor. How? Choose against him every time you see him raise his ugly head. Walk right into those situations you normally run from. Speak right to the issues you normally remain silent over. If you want to grow in true masculine strength, then you must stop sabotaging yours.

SABOTAGE

Rich is a deeply passionate young man who is really trying to learn what it means to be a man. A few weeks ago he had plans to go out with some friends. They promised to call him before they left and then come pick him up; they never called. A few days later, when one of them brought it up, Rich said, "Oh, that's okay. It's no big deal." But inside, he was *furious*. That is sabotage. He deliberately chose to push his true strength down and live the false self. Do that enough and you won't believe you have any strength. I've noticed when I deny the anger I am feeling, it turns into fear. If we will not allow what Sam Keen calls "fire in the belly," something weaker will take its place. I had a chance a few years back to tell my boss what I really thought of him; not in sinful anger (there's a difference), not to hurt him but to help him. He actually asked me to, called to see if I was free to chat for a moment. I knew what he was calling for and I ran; I told him I was busy. For days afterward I felt weak; I felt like a poser. I sabotaged my strength by refusing it.

Sabotage also happens when we give our strength away. Taking a bribe, letting yourself be bought off, accepting flattery in exchange for some sort of loyalty, is sabotage.

Refusing to confront an issue because if you keep quiet you'll get a promotion or be made an elder or keep your job corrupts you down deep. Masturbation is sabotage. It is an inherently selfish act that tears you down. I've spoken with many men whose addiction to masturbation has eroded their sense of strength. So does sexual involvement with a woman you are not married to. Carl is another young man whom the ladies seem to find especially attractive. I am astounded what young women will offer when they are famished for the love and affirmation they have never had from their fathers. They will throw themselves at a man to get a taste of being wanted, desired. Carl came to me because his sexual activity was out of control. Dozens upon dozens of women offered themselves to him and each time he gave in he felt weakened; his resolve to resist was less the next time around.

Things began to change for Carl when he saw the whole sexual struggle not so much as sin *but as a battle for his strength*. He wants to be strong, wants it desperately, and that began to fuel his choice to resist. As à Kempis said, "A man must strive long and mightily within himself, before he can learn fully to master himself." Carl and I spent hours praying through every one of those relationships, confessing the sin, breaking the bonds sexual liaisons form between two souls, cleansing his strength, asking God to restore him. He did, and I am grateful to say those days are over for Carl. It wasn't easy, but it was real; he is happily married now.

THE REAL THING

Start choosing to live out your strength and you'll discover that it grows each time. Rich was after some brakes for his car; he called the parts store and they quoted him a price of $50 for the pair. But when he got down there, the guy told him it would be $90. He was taking Rich for a fool and something in Rich was provoked. Normally he would have said "Oh, that's okay. It's no big deal," and paid the higher price; but not this time. He told the guy that the price was $50 and stood his ground. The guy backed down and stopped trying to rip him off. "It felt great," Rich told me later. "I felt that I was finally acting like a man." Now that may seem like a simple story, but this is where you will discover your strength, in the daily details of your life. Begin to taste your true strength and you'll want *more*. Something in the center of your chest feels weighty, substantial.

We must let our strength show up. It

seems so strange, after all this, that a man would not allow his strength to arrive, but many of us are unnerved by our own masculinity. What will happen if we really let it out? In *Healing the Masculine Soul*, Gordon Dalby tells a remarkable story about a man who was plagued by a recurring dream, a nightmare "in which a ferocious lion kept chasing the man until he dropped exhausted and awoke screaming." The man was dismayed; he did not know what the dream meant. Was the lion a symbol of fear? Something in his life overwhelming him? One day the man was guided by his pastor (a friend of Dalby's) to revisit the dream in prayer:

As they prayed, [the pastor] on impulse invited the man to recall the dream, even in all its fear. Hesitantly, the man agreed, and soon reported that indeed, the lion was in sight and headed his way. [The pastor] then instructed the man, "When the lion comes close to you, try not to run away, but instead, stand there and ask him who or what he is, and what he's doing in your life . . . can you try that?" Shifting uneasily in his chair, the man agreed, then reported what was happening: "The lion is snorting and shaking his head, standing right there in front of

228

me . . . I ask him who he is . . . and — Oh! I can't believe what he's saying! He says, 'I'm your courage and your strength. Why are you running away from me?' "

I had a recurring dream similar to this one for many years — especially in adolescence. A great wild stallion was standing on the ridge of a hill; I sensed danger but not an evil danger, just something strong and valiant and greater than me. I tried to sneak away; the stallion always turned in time to see me and came charging down the hill. I would wake just as he was upon me. It seems crazy that a man would sneak away from his strength, fear it to show up, but that is why we sabotage. Our strength is wild and fierce, and we are more than unsettled by what may happen if we let it arrive. One thing we know: Nothing will ever be the same. One client said to me, "I'm afraid I'll do something bad if I let all this show up." No, the opposite is true. You'll do something bad if you *don't*. Remember — a man's addictions are the result of his refusing his strength.

Years ago Brent gave me a piece of advice that changed my life: "Let people feel the weight of who you are," he said, "and let them deal with it." That brings us into the arena of our next enemy.

What is this enemy that the Scripture calls "the world"? Is it drinking and dancing and smoking? Is it going to the movies or playing cards? That is a shallow and ridiculous approach to holiness. It numbs us to the fact that good and evil are much more serious. The Scriptures never prohibit drinking alcohol, only drunkenness; dancing was a vital part of King David's life; and while there are some very godly movies out there, there are also some very ungodly churches. No, "the world" is not a place or a set of behaviors — it is any system built by our collective sin, all our false selves coming together to reward and destroy each other. Take all those posers out there, put them together in an office or a club or a church, and what you get is what the Scriptures mean by the world.

The world is a carnival of counterfeits — counterfeit battles, counterfeit adventures, counterfeit beauties. Men should think of it as a corruption of their strength. Battle your way to the top, says the world, and you are a man. Why is it then that the men who get there are often the emptiest, most frightened, prideful posers around? They are mercenaries, battling only to build their own kingdoms. There is nothing transcendent about their lives. The same holds true of the adventure addicts; no matter how much you spend, no matter how far you take your hobby, it's still merely that — a hobby. And as for the counterfeit beauties, the world is constantly trying to tell us that the Golden-Haired Woman is out there — go for her.

The world offers a man a false sense of power and a false sense of security. Be brutally honest now — where does your own sense of power come from? Is it how pretty your wife is — or your secretary? Is it how many people attend your church? Is it *knowledge* — that you have an expertise and that makes others come to you, bow to you? Is it your position, degree, or title? A white coat, a Ph.D., a podium, or a paneled office can make a man feel like pretty neat stuff. What happens inside you when I suggest you give it up? Put the book down for a few moments and consider what you would think of yourself if tomorrow you lost everything that the world has rewarded you for. "Without Christ a man must fail miserably," says MacDonald, "or succeed even more miserably." Jesus warns us against anything that gives a false sense of power. When you walk into a company dinner or a church function, he said, take a backseat.

Choose the path of humility; don't be a self-promoter, a glad-hander, a poser. Climb *down* the ladder; have the mail clerk over for dinner; treat your secretary like she's more important than you; look to be the servant of all. *Where am I deriving my sense of strength and power from?* is a good question to ask yourself . . . often.

If you want to know how the world *really* feels about you, just start living out of your true strength. Say what you think, stand up for the underdog, challenge foolish policies. They'll turn on you like sharks. Remember the film *Jerry McGuire*? Jerry is an agent for professional athletes who comes to a sort of personal epiphany about the corruption of his firm. He issues a memo, a vision statement urging a more humane approach to their work. Let's stop treating people like cattle, he says; stop serving the bottom line and really serve our clients. All his buddies cheer him on; when the firm dumps him (as he knew they would) they rush to seize his clients. I've seen this time and time again. A friend of mine confronted his pastor on some false statements the pastor had made to get his position. This shepherd of the flock started circulating rumors that my friend was gay; he tried to ruin his reputation.

The world of posers is shaken by a real

man. They'll do whatever it takes to get you back in line — threaten you, bribe you, seduce you, undermine you. They crucified Jesus. But it didn't work, did it? You must let your strength show up. Remember Christ in the Garden, the sheer force of his presence? Many of us have actually been afraid to let our strength show up because the world doesn't have a place for it. Fine. The world's screwed up. Let people feel the weight of who you are and let them deal with it.

THE DEVIL

My wife and I were driving home the other day from an afternoon out and running a bit late to get to our son's last soccer game of the season. I was in the driver's seat and we were enjoying a lingering conversation about some dreams we have for the future. After several minutes we realized that we were caught in a traffic jam that was going nowhere. Precious moments slipped by as tension mounted in the car. In an effort to be helpful, Stasi suggested an alternate route: "If you take a right here and go up to First Street, we can cut over and take about five minutes off the drive." I was ready to divorce her. I'm serious. In about twenty seconds I was ready for separation. If the judge had been in the car, I'd have signed the papers right there. Good grief — over a comment about my driving? Is that all that was going on in that moment?

I sat at the wheel silent and steaming. On the outside, I looked cool; inside, here is what was happening: *Geez, doesn't she think I know how to get there? I hate it when she does that.* Then another voice says, *She always does that.* And I say (internally — the whole dialogue took place internally, in the blink of an eye), *Yeah, she does . . . she's always saying stuff like that. I hate that about her.* A feeling of accusation and anger and self-righteousness sweeps over me. Then the voice says, *John, this is never going to change,* and I say, *This is never going to change,* and the voice says, *You know, John, there are a lot of women out there who would be deeply grateful to have you as their man,* and I think, *Yeah — there are a lot of women out there . . .* You get the picture. Change the characters and the setting and the very same thing has happened to you. Only, you probably thought the whole thing was your own mess.

The devil no doubt has a place in our theology, but is he a category we even think about in the daily events of our lives? Has it ever crossed your mind that not every thought that crosses your mind comes from you? What I experienced in the midst of traffic that day happens all the time in marriages, in ministries, in any relationship. We are being lied to all the time. Yet we never stop to say, "Wait a minute . . . who else is speaking here? Where are those ideas coming from? Where are those *feelings* coming from?" If you read the saints from every age before the Modern Era — that pride-filled age of reason, science, and technology we all were thoroughly educated in — you'll find that they take the devil very seriously indeed. As Paul says, "We are not unaware of his schemes" (2 Cor. 2:11). But we, the enlightened, have a much more commonsense approach to things. We look for a psychological or physical or even political explanation for every trouble we meet.

Who caused the Chaldeans to steal Job's herds and kill his servants? Satan, clearly (Job 1:12, 17). Yet do we even give him a passing thought when we hear of terrorism today? Who kept that poor woman bent over for eighteen years, the one Jesus healed on the Sabbath? Satan, clearly (Luke 13:16). But do we consider him when we are having a headache that keeps us from praying or reading Scripture? Who moved Ananias and Sapphira to lie to the apostles?

Satan again (Acts 5:3). But do we really see his hand behind a fallout or schism in ministry? Who was behind that brutal assault on your own strength, those wounds you've taken? As William Gurnall said, "It is the image of God reflected in you that so enrages hell; it is this at which the demons hurl their mightiest weapons."

There is a whole lot more going on behind the scenes of our lives than most of us have been led to believe. Take Christmas for example.

BEHIND THE SCENES

Most of you probably have a Nativity scene that you take out over the holidays and place on a mantel or coffee table. Most of these scenes share a regular cast of characters: shepherds, wise men, maybe a few barnyard animals, Joseph, Mary, and, of course, the baby Jesus. Yes, ours has an angel or two and I imagine yours does as well. But that's about as far as the supernatural gets. What is the overall *mood* of the scene? Don't they all have a sort of warm, pastoral atmosphere to them, a quiet, intimate feel like the one you get when you sing *Silent Night* or *Away in a Manger*? And while that's all very true, it is also very *deceiving* because it is not a full picture of what's really going on. For that, you have to turn to Revelation 12:

> A great and wondrous sign appeared in heaven: a woman clothed with the sun, with the moon under her feet and a crown of twelve stars on her head. She was pregnant and cried out in pain as she was about to give birth. Then another sign appeared in heaven: an enormous red dragon with seven heads and ten horns and seven crowns on his heads. His tail swept a third of the stars out of the sky and flung them to the earth. The dragon stood in front of the woman who was about to give birth, so that he might devour her child the moment it was born. She gave birth to a son, a male child, who will rule all the nations with an iron scepter . . . And there was war in heaven. Michael and his angels fought against the dragon, and the dragon and his angels fought back. But he was not strong enough, and they lost their place in heaven. The great dragon was hurled down — that ancient serpent called the devil or Satan, who leads the whole world astray. He was hurled to the earth, and his angels with him. (vv. 1–5, 7–9)

As Philip Yancey says, I have never seen this version of the story on a Christmas card. Yet it is the truer story, the rest of the picture of what was going on that fateful night. Yancey calls the birth of Christ the Great Invasion, "a daring raid by the ruler of the forces of good into the universe's seat of evil." Spiritually speaking, this is no silent night. It is D-Day. "It is almost beyond my comprehension too, and yet I accept that this notion is the key to understanding Christmas and is, in fact, the touchstone of my faith. As a Christian I believe that we live in parallel worlds. One world consists of hills and lakes and barns and politicians and shepherds watching their flocks by night. The other consists of angels and sinister forces" and the whole spiritual realm. The child is born, the woman escapes and the story continues like this:

Then the dragon was enraged at the woman and went off to make war against the rest of her offspring — those who obey God's commandments and hold to the testimony of Jesus. (Rev. 12:17)

Behind the world and the flesh is an even more deadly enemy . . . one we rarely speak of and are even much less ready to resist. Yet this is where we live now — on the front lines of a fierce spiritual war that is to blame for most of the casualties you see around you and most of the assault against you. It's time we prepared ourselves for it. Yes, Luke, there is a dragon. Here is how you slay him.

Chapter Nine

A BATTLE TO FIGHT: THE STRATEGY

She was right that reality can be harsh and that you shut your eyes to it only at your peril because if you do not face up to the enemy in all his dark power, then the enemy will come up from behind some dark day and destroy you while you are facing the other way.

— FREDERICK BUECHNER

Gird your sword upon your side, O mighty one, clothe yourself with splendor and majesty.
In your majesty ride forth victoriously.

— PSALM 45:3–4

As part of Christ's army, you march in the ranks of gallant spirits. Every one of your fellow soldiers is the child of a King. Some, like you, are in the midst of battle, besieged on every side by affliction and temptation. Others, after many assaults, repulses, and rallyings of their faith, are already

standing upon the wall of heaven as conquerors. From there they look down and urge you, their comrades on earth, to march up the hill after them. This is their cry: "Fight to the death and the City is your own, as now it is ours!"
— WILLIAM GURNALL

The invasion of France and the end of WWII actually began the night before the Allies hit the beaches at Normandy, when the 82nd and 101st Airborne Divisions were dropped in behind enemy lines to cut off Hitler's reinforcements. If you've seen *The Longest Day* or *Saving Private Ryan*, you remember the dangers those paratroopers were facing. Alone or in small groups, they moved through the dead of night across a country they had never been to in order to fight an enemy they couldn't see or predict. It was a moment of unparalleled bravery . . . and cowardice. For not every trooper played the man that fateful night. Sure, they jumped; but afterward, many hid. One group took cowardice to a new level.

Too many had hunkered down in hedgerows to await the dawn; a few had even gone to sleep. Pvt. Francis Palys of the 506th saw what was perhaps the worst dereliction of duty. He had gathered a squad near Vierville. Hearing "all kinds of noise and singing from a distance," he and his men sneaked up on a farmhouse. In it was a mixed group from both American divisions. The paratroopers had found [liquor] in the cellar . . . and they were drunker than a bunch of hillbillies on a Saturday night wingding. Unbelievable. (*D-Day*)

Unbelievable indeed. These men *knew* they were at war, yet they refused to act like it. They lived in a dangerous denial — a denial that not only endangered them but countless others who depended on them to do their part. It is a *perfect* picture of the church in the West when it comes to spiritual warfare. During a recent church staff meeting, a friend of mine raised the suggestion that some of the difficulties they were facing might be the work of the Enemy. "What do you think?" he asked. "Well, I suppose that sort of thing does happen," one of the other pastors replied. "In the Third World, perhaps, or maybe to thwart a major crusade. You know . . . places where cutting-edge ministry is going on."

STAGE ONE: "I'M NOT HERE"

Incredible. What a self-indictment. "Nothing dangerous is happening here." Those men have already been taken out because they've swallowed the Enemy's first line of attack: "I'm not here — this is all just you." You can't fight a battle you don't think exists. This is right out of *The Screwtape*

Letters, where Lewis has the old devil instruct his apprentice in this very matter:

> My dear Wormwood, I wonder you should ask me whether it is essential to keep the patient in ignorance of your own existence. That question, at least for the present phase of the struggle, has been answered for us by the High Command. Our policy, for the moment, is to conceal ourselves.

As for those who want to be dangerous (cutting-edge), take a close look at 1 Peter 5:8–9: "Be self-controlled and alert. Your enemy the devil prowls around like a roaring lion looking for someone to devour. Resist him, standing firm in the faith, because you know that your brothers throughout the world are undergoing the same kind of sufferings." What is the Holy Spirit, through Peter, assuming about your life? *That you are under spiritual attack.* This is not a passage about nonbelievers; he's talking about "your brethren." Peter takes it for granted that every believer is under some sort of unseen assault. And what does he insist you do? *Resist* the devil. Fight back, take a stand.

A ministry partnership that some dear friends were central to has just dissolved this week, I am deeply sad to say. They had teamed up with another organization to bring the gospel to cities across the U.S. These conferences are very powerful; in fact, I've never seen anything even close to the impact they have. Through grateful tears, the attendees talk about the healing, the freedom, the release they have experienced. They recover their hearts and are drawn into an intimacy with God most have never, ever experienced before. It's beautiful and awe-inspiring. Now, do you think the Enemy just lets that sort of thing go swimmingly along without any interference whatsoever?

The partnership hit some choppy water, nothing much at all really, nothing unusual to any relationship, yet the other members simply decided to end the coalition and walk away mid-season. Were there personal issues involved? You bet; there always are. But they were minor. It was mostly misunderstanding and injured pride. There was not one word, not one thought as far as I could tell about the Enemy and what he might be doing to break up so strategic an alliance. When I brought up the fact that they would do well to interpret things with open eyes, keeping the attacks of the Evil One in mind, I was dismissed. These good people with good hearts wanted to explain everything on a "human" level and let me tell you — when you ignore the Enemy, he wins. He simply loves to blame everything on us, get us feeling hurt, misunderstood, suspicious, and resentful of one another.

Before an effective military strike can be made, you must take out the opposing army's line of communication. The Evil One does this all the time — in ministries and especially between couples. Marriage is a stunning picture of what God offers his people. Scripture tells us it is a living metaphor, a walking parable, a Rembrandt painting of the gospel. The Enemy knows this, *and he hates it* with every ounce of his malicious heart. He has no intention of just letting that beautiful portrait be lived out before the world with such deep appeal that no one can resist God's offer. So just like in the Garden, Satan comes in to divide and conquer. Often I'll feel this sense of accusation when I'm with my wife. It's hard to describe and it usually isn't put into words, but I just receive this message that *I'm blowing it.* I finally brought this up with Stasi and tears came to her eyes. "You're kidding," she said. "I've been feeling the very same thing. I thought you were disappointed with *me.*" Wait a minute, I thought.

If I'm not sending this message and you're not sending this message . . .

Most of all the Enemy will try to jam communications with Headquarters. Commit yourself to prayer every morning for two weeks and just watch what'll happen. You won't want to get up; an important meeting will be called that interferes; you'll catch a cold; or, if you do get to your prayers, your mind will wander to what you'll have for breakfast and how much you should pay for that water heater repair and what color socks would look best with your gray suit. Many, many times I've simply come under a cloak of *confusion* so thick I suddenly find myself wondering why I ever believed in Jesus in the first place. That sweet communion I normally enjoy with God is cut off, gone, vanished like the sun behind a cloud. If you don't know what's up you'll think you really have lost your faith or been abandoned by God or whatever spin the Enemy puts on it. Oswald Chambers warns us, "Sometimes there is nothing to obey, the only thing to do is to maintain a vital connection with Jesus Christ, to see that nothing interferes with that."

Next comes propaganda. Like the infamous Tokyo Rose, the Enemy is constantly broadcasting messages to try to demoralize us. As in my episode during the traffic jam, he is constantly *putting his spin* on things. After all, Scripture calls him the "accuser of our brethren" (Rev. 12:10 NKJV). Think of what goes on — what you hear and feel — when you really blow it. *I'm such an idiot, I always do that, I'll never amount to anything.* Sounds like accusation to me. How about when you're really trying to step forward as a man? I can guarantee you what will happen when I'm going to speak. I was driving to the airport for a trip to the West Coast, to give a talk to men about *Wild at Heart.* All the way there I was under this cloud of heaviness; I was nearly overcome by a deep sense of *John, you're such a poser. You have absolutely nothing to say. Just turn the car around, go home, and tell them you can't make it.* Now in my clearer moments I know it's an attack, but you must understand that all this comes on so subtly it seems true at the time. I nearly gave in and went home.

When Christ is assaulted by the Evil One in the wilderness, the attack is ultimately on his identity. "*If* you are the Son of God," Satan sneers three times, then prove it (Luke 4:1–13). Brad returned from the mission field last year for a sabbatical. After seven years abroad, most of the time without any real companionship, he was pretty beat up; he felt like a failure. He told me that when he woke in the morning he'd "hear" a voice in his thoughts say, *Good morning . . . Loser.* So many men live under a similar accusation. Craig had really been entering into the battle and fighting bravely the past several months. Then he had a nightmare, a very vivid, grisly dream in which he had molested a little girl. He woke up feeling filthy and condemned. That same week I had a dream where I was accused of committing adultery; I really hadn't, but in my dream no one would believe me. Follow this: So long as a man remains no real threat to the Enemy, Satan's line to him is *You're fine.* But after you do take sides, it becomes *Your heart is bad and you know it.*

Finally, he probes the perimeter, looking for a weakness. Here's how this works: Satan will throw a thought or a temptation at us in hopes that we will swallow it. He knows your story, knows what works with you and so the line is tailor-made to your situation. Just this morning in my prayer time it was pride, then worry, then adultery, then greed, then gluttony. If I thought this was all me, my heart, I'd be very discouraged. Knowing that my heart is good allowed me to block it, right then and there. When

Satan probes, make no agreements. If we make an agreement, if something in our heart says, *Yeah, you're right,* then he pours it on. You'll see a beautiful woman and something in you will say, *You want her.* That's the Evil One appealing to the traitor within. If the traitor says, *Yes, I do,* then the lust really begins to take hold. Let that go on for years and you've given him a stronghold. This can make a good man feel so awful because he thinks he's a lustful man when he's not; it's an attack through and through.

Please don't misunderstand me. I'm not blaming everything on the devil. In almost every situation there are human issues involved. Every man has his struggles; every marriage has its rough spots; every ministry has personal conflicts. But those issues are like a campfire that the Enemy throws gasoline all over and turns into a bonfire. The flames leap up into a raging inferno and we are suddenly overwhelmed with what we're feeling. Simple misunderstandings become grounds for divorce. All the while we believe that it's us, we are blowing it, we're to blame, and the Enemy is laughing because we've swallowed the lie "I'm not here, it's just you." We've got to be a lot more cunning than that.

HANGING ON TO THE TRUTH

In any hand-to-hand combat, there's a constant back-and-forth of blows, dodges, blocks, counterattacks, and so forth. That's exactly what is going on in the unseen around us. Only it takes place, initially, at the level of our thoughts. When we are under attack, we've got to hang on to the truth. Dodge the blow, block it with a stubborn refusal, slash back with what is true. This is how Christ answered Satan — he didn't get into an argument with him, try to reason his way out. He simply stood on the truth. He answered with Scripture and we've got to do the same. This will not be easy, especially when all hell is breaking loose around you. It will feel like holding on to a rope while you're being dragged behind a truck, like keeping your balance in a hurricane. Satan doesn't just throw a thought at us; he throws *feelings* too. Walk into a dark house late at night and suddenly fear sweeps over you; or just stand in a grocery line with all those tabloids shouting sex at you and suddenly a sense of corruption is yours.

But this is where your strength is revealed and even increased — through exercise. Stand on what is true and do not let go. Period. The traitor within the castle will try to lower the drawbridge but don't let him. When Proverbs 4:23 tells us to guard our hearts, it's not saying, "Lock them up because they're really criminal to the core"; it's saying, "Defend them like a castle, the seat of your strength you do not want to give away." As à Kempis says, "Yet we must be watchful, especially in the beginning of the temptation; for the enemy is then more easily overcome, if he is not suffered to enter the door of our hearts, but is resisted without the gate at his first knock."

Remember the scene in *Braveheart* where Robert the Bruce's evil father is whispering lies to him about treason and compromise? He says to Robert what the Enemy says to us in a thousand ways: "All men betray; all men lose heart." How does Robert answer? He yells back,

I don't want to lose heart!
I want to believe, like [Wallace] does.
I will never be on the wrong side again.

That is the turning point in his life . . . and in ours. The battle shifts to a new level.

STAGE TWO: INTIMIDATION

Stasi lived under a cloud of depression for many years. We had seen her find some healing through counseling, but still the depression remained. We had addressed the physical aspects that we could through medication, yet it lingered still. *Okay,* I thought to myself, *the Bible tells me that we have a body, a soul, and a spirit. We've addressed the body and soul issues . . . what's left must be spiritual.* Stasi and I began to read a bit on dealing with the Enemy. In the course of our study she came across a passage that referred to different symptoms that sometimes accompany depression; one of them was dizziness. As she read the passage out loud she sounded surprised. "What about it?" I asked. "Well . . . I get dizzy spells a lot." "Really? How often?" "Oh, every day." "Every day??!!" I had been married to Stasi for ten years and she had never even mentioned this to me. The poor woman had simply thought they were normal for everyone since they were normal for her.

"Stasi, I have never had a dizzy spell in my life. I think we're onto something here." We began to pray against the dizziness, taking authority over any attack in the name of Jesus. You know what happened? It got *worse!* The Enemy, once discovered, usually doesn't just roll over and go away without a fight. Notice that sometimes Jesus rebukes a foul spirit "in a stern voice" (see Luke 4:35). In fact, when he encounters the guy who lives out in the Gerasenes tombs, tormented by a legion of spirits, the first rebuke by Jesus doesn't work. He had to get more information, really take them on (Luke 8:26–33). Now if Jesus had to get tough with these guys, don't you suppose we'll have to as well? Stasi and I held our ground, resisting the onslaught "firm in the faith," as Peter says, and you know what? The dizzy spells ended. They are history. She hasn't had one for seven years.

That is the next level of our Enemy's strategy. When we begin to question him, to resist his lies, to see his hand in the "ordinary trials" of our lives, then he steps up the attack; he turns to intimidation and fear. In fact, at some point in the last several pages you've probably begun to feel something like *Do I really want to get into all this superspiritual hocus-pocus? It's kind of creepy anyway*. Satan will try to get you to agree with intimidation *because he fears you*. You are a huge threat to him. He doesn't want you waking up and fighting back because when you do he loses. "Resist the devil," James says, *"and he will flee from you"* (James

254

4:7, emphasis added). So he's going to try to keep you from taking a stand. He moves from subtle seduction to open assault. The thoughts come crashing in, all sorts of stuff begins to fall apart in your life, your faith seems paper thin.

Why do so many pastors' kids go off the deep end? You think that's a coincidence? So many churches start off with life and vitality only to end in a split, or simply wither away and die. How come? Why did a friend of mine nearly black out when she tried to share her testimony at a meeting? Why are my flights so often thwarted when I'm trying to take the gospel to a city? Why does everything seem to fall apart at work when you're making some advances at home, or vice versa? Because we are at war and the Evil One is trying an old tactic — strike first and maybe the opposition will turn tail and run. He can't win, you know. As Franklin Roosevelt said, "We have nothing to fear but fear itself."

GOD IS WITH US

Be strong and courageous, because you will lead these people to inherit the land I swore to their forefathers to give them. Be strong and very courageous . . . Have

I not commanded you? Be strong and courageous. Do not be terrified; do not be discouraged, for the LORD your God will be with you wherever you go. (Josh. 1:6–7, 9)

Joshua knew what it was to be afraid. For years he had been second in command, Moses' right-hand man. But now it was his turn to lead. The children of Israel weren't just going to waltz in and pick up the promised land like a quart of milk; they were going to have to fight for it. And Moses was not going with them. If Joshua was completely confident about the situation, why would God have had to tell him over and over and over again not to be afraid? In fact, God gives him a special word of encouragement: "As I was with Moses, so I will be with you; I will never leave you nor forsake you" (Josh. 1:5). How was God "with Moses"? As a mighty warrior. Remember the plagues? Remember all those Egyptian soldiers drowned with their horses and chariots out there in the Red Sea? It was after that display of God's strength that the people of Israel sang, "The LORD is a warrior; the LORD is his name" (Ex. 15:3). God fought for Moses and for Israel; then he covenanted to

Joshua to do the same and they took down Jericho and every other enemy.

Jeremiah knew what it meant to have God "with him" as well. "But the Lord is with me like a mighty warrior," he sang. "So my persecutors will stumble and not prevail" (Jer. 20:11). Even Jesus walked in this promise when he battled for us here on earth:

> You know what has happened throughout Judea, beginning in Galilee after the baptism that John preached — how God anointed Jesus of Nazareth with the Holy Spirit and power, and how he went around doing good and healing all who were under the power of the devil, *because God was with him.* (Acts 10:37–38, emphasis added)

How did Jesus win the battle against Satan? God was *with him.* This really opens up the riches of the promise Christ gives us when he pledges "I am with you always, even to the end of the age" and "I will never leave you nor forsake you" (Matt. 28:20; Heb. 13:5 NKJV). That doesn't simply mean that he'll be around, or even that he'll comfort us in our afflictions. It means *he will fight for us,* with us, just as he has fought for his people all through the ages. So long as we walk with Christ, stay in him, we haven't a thing to fear.

Satan is trying to appeal to the traitor's commitment to self-preservation when he uses fear and intimidation. So long as we are back in the old story of saving our skin, looking out for Number One, those tactics will work. We'll shrink back. But the opposite is also true. When a man resolves to become a warrior, when his life is given over to a transcendent cause, then he can't be cowed by the Big Bad Wolf threatening to blow his house down. After Revelation describes that war in heaven between the angels and Satan's downfall to the earth, it tells how the saints overcame him:

> They overcame him
> by the blood of the Lamb
> and by the word of their testimony;
> they did not love their lives so much
> as to shrink from death. (12:11)

The most dangerous man on earth is the man who has reckoned with his own death. All men die; few men ever really *live*. Sure, you can create a safe life for yourself . . . and end your days in a rest home babbling on about some forgotten misfortune. I'd rather go down swinging. Besides, the less we are trying to "save ourselves," the more effective a warrior we will be. Listen to G. K. Chesterton on courage:

> Courage is almost a contradiction in terms. It means a strong desire to live taking the form of a readiness to die. "He that will lose his life, the same shall save it," is not a piece of mysticism for saints and heroes. It is a piece of everyday advice for sailors or mountaineers. It might be printed in an Alpine guide or a drill book. The paradox is the whole principle of courage; even of quite earthly or quite brutal courage. A man cut off by the sea may save his life if he will risk it on the precipice. He can only get away from death by continually stepping within an inch of it. A soldier surrounded by enemies, if he is to cut his way out, needs to combine a strong desire for living with a strange carelessness about dying. He must not merely cling to live, for then he will be a coward, and will not escape. He must not merely wait for death, for then he will be a suicide, and will not escape. He must seek his life in a spirit of furious indifference

to it; he must desire life like water and yet drink death like wine.

STAGE THREE: CUTTING A DEAL

The third level of attack the Evil One employs, after we have resisted deception and intimidation, is simply to try to get us to cut a deal. So many men have been bought off in one way or another. The phone just rang; a friend called to tell me that yet another Christian leader has fallen into sexual immorality. The church wags its head and says, "You see. He just couldn't keep himself clean." That is naive. Do you think that man, a follower of Christ, in his heart of hearts really *wanted* to fall? What man begins his journey wishing, "I think one day, after twenty years of ministry, I'll torpedo the whole thing with an affair"? He was *picked off;* the whole thing was plotted. In his case it was a long and subtle assignment to wear his defenses down not so much through battle as through *boredom.* I knew that man; he had no great cause to fight for, just the monotony of "professional Christian ministry" that he hated but couldn't get out of because he was being so well paid for it. He was set up for a fall. Unless you are aware that that's what it is, you'll be taken out too.

Notice this — when did King David fall? What were the circumstances of his affair with Bathsheba? "In the spring, at the time when kings go off to war, David sent Joab out with the king's men and the whole Israelite army" (2 Sam. 11:1). David was no longer a warrior; he sent others to do his fighting for him. Bored, sated, and fat, he strolls around on the roof of the palace looking for something to amuse him. The Evil One points out Bathsheba and the rest is history — which, as we all know, repeats itself. William Gurnall warns us,

Persisting to the end will be the burr under your saddle — the thorn in your flesh — when the road ahead seems endless and your soul begs an early discharge. It weighs down every other difficulty of your calling. We have known many who have joined the army of Christ and like being a soldier for a battle or two, but have soon had enough and ended up deserting. They impulsively enlist for Christian duties . . . and are just as easily persuaded to lay it down. Like the new moon, they shine a little in the first part of the evening, but go down before the night is over. (*The Christian in Full Armor*)

Against the flesh, the traitor within, a warrior uses discipline. We have a two-dimensional version of this now, which we call a "quiet time." But most men have a hard time sustaining any sort of devotional life because it has no vital connection to recovering and protecting their strength; it feels about as important as flossing. But if you saw your life as a great battle and you *knew* you needed time with God for your very survival, you would do it. Maybe not perfectly — nobody ever does and that's not the point anyway — but you would have a reason to seek him. We give a half-hearted attempt at the spiritual disciplines when the only reason we have is that we "ought" to. But we'll find a way to make it work when we are convinced we're history if we don't.

Time with God each day is not about academic study or getting through a certain amount of Scripture or any of that. It's about connecting with God. We've got to keep those lines of communication open, so use whatever helps. Sometimes I'll listen to music; other times I'll read Scripture or a passage from a book; often I will journal; maybe I'll go for a run; then there are days when all I need is silence and solitude and the rising sun. The point is simply to do *whatever brings me back to my heart and the heart of God.* God has spared me many times from an ambush I had no idea was coming; he warned me in my time with him in the early morning about something that was going to happen that day. Just the other day it was a passage from a book about forgiveness. I sensed he was saying something to me personally. *Lord, am I unforgiving? No,* he said. About an hour later I received a very painful phone call — a betrayal. *Oh, you were telling me to be ready to forgive, weren't you? Yes.*

The discipline, by the way, is never the point. The whole point of a "devotional life" is *connecting with God.* This is our primary antidote to the counterfeits the world holds out to us. If you do not have God and have him deeply, you will turn to other lovers. As Maurice Roberts says,

Ecstasy and delight are essential to the believer's soul and they promote sanctification. We are not meant to live without spiritual exhilaration . . . The believer is in spiritual danger if he allows himself to go for any length of time without tasting the love of Christ . . . When Christ ceases to fill the heart with

263

satisfaction, our souls will go in silent search of other lovers. (*The Thought of God*)

A man will devote long hours to his finances when he has a goal of an early retirement; he'll endure rigorous training when he aims to run a 10k or even a marathon. The ability to discipline himself is there, but dormant for many of us. "When a warrior is in service, however, to a True King — that is, to a transcendent cause," says Bly, "he does well, and his body becomes a hardworking servant, which he requires to endure cold, heat, pain, wounds, scarring, hunger, lack of sleep, hardship of all kinds, do what is necessary."

Against the Evil One we wear the armor of God. That God has provided weapons of war for us sure makes a lot more sense if our days are like a scene from *Saving Private Ryan*. How many Christians have read over those passages about the shield of faith and the helmet of salvation and never really known what to do with them. *What lovely poetic imagery; I wonder what it means.* It means that God has given you armor and you'd better put it on. Every day. This equipment is really there, in the spiritual, unseen realm. We don't see it, but the angels and our enemies do. Start by simply praying through the passage in Ephesians as if suiting up for the arena:

"Therefore put on the full armor of God, so that when the day of evil comes, you may be able to stand your ground, and after you have done everything, to stand. Stand firm then, with the belt of truth buckled around your waist . . ." *Lord, I put on the belt of truth. I choose a lifestyle of honesty and integrity. Show me the truths I so desperately need today. Expose the lies I'm not even aware that I'm believing.* ". . . with the breastplate of righteousness in place . . ." *And yes, Lord, I wear your righteousness today against all condemnation and corruption. Fit me with your holiness and purity — defend me from all assaults against my heart.* ". . . and with your feet fitted with the readiness that comes from the gospel of peace . . ." *I do choose to live for the gospel at any moment. Show me where the larger story is unfolding and keep me from being so lax that I think the most important thing today is the soap operas of this world.*

"In addition to all this, take up the shield of faith, with which you can extinguish all the flaming arrows of the evil one . . ." *Jesus, I lift against every lie and every assault the confidence that you are good, and that you have good in store for me. Nothing is coming today that can overcome me because you are with me.* ". . . Take the helmet of salvation . . ." *Thank you, Lord, for my salvation. I receive it in a new and fresh way from you and I declare that nothing can separate me now from the love of Christ and the place I shall ever have in your kingdom.* ". . . and the sword of the Spirit, which is the word of God . . ." *Holy Spirit, show me specifically today the truths of the Word of God that I will need to counter the assaults and the snares of the Enemy. Bring them to mind throughout the day.* ". . . And pray in the Spirit on all occasions with all kinds of prayers and requests. With this in mind, be alert and always keep on praying for all the saints." *Finally, Holy Spirit, I agree to walk in step with you in everything — in all prayer as my spirit communes with you throughout the day.* (6:13–18)

And we walk in the authority of Christ. Do not attack in anger, do not swagger forth in pride. You will get nailed. I love the scene in *The Mask of Zorro* when the old master swordsman saves his young apprentice — who at that moment has had too much to drink — from rushing upon his enemy. "You would have fought bravely," he says, "and died quickly." All authority in heaven and on earth has been given to Jesus Christ (Matt. 28:18). He tells us this before he gives us the Great Commission, the command to advance his kingdom. Why? We've never made the connection. The reason is, if you are going to serve the True King you're going to need his authority. We dare not take on any angel, let alone a fallen one, in our own strength. That is why Christ extends his authority to us, "and you have been given fullness in Christ, who is the head over every power and authority" (Col. 2:10). Rebuke the Enemy in your own name and he laughs; command him in the name of Christ and he flees.

One more thing: Don't even think about going into battle alone. Don't even try to take the masculine journey without at least one man by your side. Yes, there are times a man must face the battle alone, in the wee hours of the morn, and fight with all he's got. But don't make that a lifestyle of isolation. This may be our weakest point, as David Smith points out in *The Friendless American Male*: "One serious problem is the friendless condition of the average American male. Men find it hard to accept that they need the fellowship of other men." Thanks to the men's movement the church understands now that a man needs other men, but what we've offered is another two-dimensional solution: "Accountability" groups or partners. Ugh. That sounds so old covenant: "You're really a fool and you're just waiting to rush into sin, so we'd better post a guard by you to keep you in line."

We don't need accountability groups; we need fellow warriors, someone to fight alongside, someone to watch our back. A young man just stopped me on the street to say, "I feel surrounded by enemies and I'm all alone." The whole crisis in masculinity today has come because we no longer have a warrior culture, a place for men to learn to fight like men. We don't need a meeting of Really Nice Guys; we need a gathering of Really Dangerous Men. *That's* what we need. I think of Henry V at Agincourt. His army has been reduced to a small band of tired and weary men; many of them are wounded. They are outnumbered five to one. But Henry rallies his troops to his side when he reminds them that they are not mercenaries, but a "band of brothers."

We few, we happy few, we band of
   brothers;
For he to-day that sheds his blood
   with me
Shall be my brother . . .
And gentlemen in England, now a-
   bed
Shall think themselves accursed they
   were not here;
And hold their manhoods cheap
   whiles any speaks
That fought with us.

Yes, we need men to whom we can bare our souls. But it isn't going to happen with a group of guys you don't trust, who really aren't willing to go to battle with you. It's a long-standing truth that there is never a more devoted group of men than those who have fought alongside one another, the men of your squadron, the guys in your foxhole. It will never be a large group, but we don't need a large group. We need a band of brothers willing to "shed their blood" with us.

HONOR WOUNDS

A warning before we leave this chapter: You will be wounded. Just because this battle is spiritual doesn't mean it's not real; it is, and the wounds a man can take are in some ways more ugly than those that come in a firefight. To lose a leg is nothing compared to losing heart; to be crippled by shrapnel need not destroy your soul, but to be crippled by shame and guilt may. You will be wounded by the Enemy. He knows the wounds of your past, and he will try to wound you again in the same place. But these wounds are different; these are honor-wounds. As Rick Joyner says, "It is an honor to be wounded in the service of the Lord."

Blaine was showing me his scars the other night at the dinner table. "This one is where Samuel threw a rock and hit me in the forehead. And this one is from the Tetons when I fell into that sharp log. I can't remember what this one was from; oh, here's a good one — this one is from when I fell into the pond while chasing Luke. This one is a really old one when I burned my leg on the stove camping." He's proud of his scars; they are badges of honor to a boy . . . and to a man. We have no equivalent now for a Purple Heart of spiritual warfare, but we will. One of the noblest moments that await us will come at the Wedding Feast of the Lamb. Our Lord will rise and begin to call those forward who were wounded in battle for his name's sake and they will be honored, their courage rewarded. I think of Henry V's line to his men,

> He that outlives this day, and comes safe home,
> Will stand a tip-toe when the day is named,
> And rouse him at the name of Crispian . . .
> Then will he strip his sleeve and show his scars,
> And say, "These wounds I had on Crispin's day."
> Old men forget; yet all shall be forgot,
> But he'll remember with advantages
> What feats he did that day; then shall our names . . .
> Be in their flowing cups freshly remember'd.

"The kingdom of heaven suffers violence," said Jesus, "and violent men take it by force" (Matt, 11: 12 NASB). Is that a good thing or a bad thing? Hopefully by now you see the deep and holy goodness of masculine aggression and that will help you understand what Christ is saying. Contrast it with this: "The kingdom of heaven is open to passive, wimpy men who enter it by lying on the couch watching TV." If you are

271

going to live in God's kingdom, Jesus says, it's going to take every ounce of passion and forcefulness you've got. Things are going to get fierce; that's why you were given a fierce heart. I love the image of this verse given to us by John Bunyan in *Pilgrim's Progress*:

Then the Interpreter took [Christian] and led him up toward the door of the palace; and behold, at the door stood a great company of men, as desirous to go in, but [dared] not. There also sat a man at a little distance from the door, at a tableside, with a book and his inkhorn before him, to take the names of them that should enter therein; he saw also that in the doorway stood many men in armor to keep it, being resolved to do the men that would enter what hurt and mischief they could. Now was Christian somewhat in amaze. At last, when every man [fell] back for fear of the armed men, Christian saw a man of a very stout countenance come up to the man that sat there to write, saying, "Set down my name, sir," the which when he had done, he saw the man draw his sword, and put a helmet upon his head, and rush toward the door upon the armed men, who laid upon him with deadly force; but the

man, not at all discouraged, fell to cutting and hacking most fiercely. So after
he had received and given many wounds
to those that attempted to keep him out,
he cut his way through them all, and
pressed forward into the palace.

Chapter Ten

A BEAUTY TO RESCUE

Beauty is not only a terrible thing, it is also a mysterious thing. There God and the Devil strive for mastery, and the battleground is the heart of men.

— FYODOR DOSTOYEVSKY

*You'll be glad every night
That you treated her right.*

— GEORGE THOROGOOD
"Treat Her Right"
by Roy Head
and Gene Kurtz

*Cowboy take me away
Closer to heaven and closer to you.*

— DIXIE CHICKS
"Cowboy Take Me Away"
(© 1999 by Martie Seidel
and Marcus Hummon)

Once upon a time (as the story goes) there was a beautiful maiden, an absolute enchantress. She might be the daughter of a king or a common servant girl, but we know she is a princess at heart. She is young with a youth that seems eternal. Her flowing hair, her deep eyes, her luscious lips, her sculpted figure — she makes the rose blush for shame; the sun is pale compared to her light. Her heart is golden, her love as true as an arrow. But this lovely maiden is unattainable, the prisoner of an evil power who holds her captive in a dark tower. Only a champion may win her; only the most valiant, daring, and brave warrior has a chance of setting her free. Against all hope he comes; with cunning and raw courage he lays siege to the tower and the sinister one who holds her. Much blood is shed on both sides; three times the knight is thrown back, but three times he rises again. Eventually the sorcerer is defeated; the dragon falls, the giant is slain. The maiden is his; through his valor he has won her heart. On horseback they ride off to his cottage by a stream in the woods for a rendezvous that gives passion and romance new meaning.

Why is this story so deep in our psyche? Every little girl knows the fable without ever being told. She dreams one day her prince will come. Little boys rehearse their part with wooden swords and cardboard shields. And one day the boy, now a young man, realizes that he wants to be the one to win the beauty. Fairy tales, literature, music, and movies all borrow from this mythic theme. Sleeping Beauty, Cinderella, Helen of Troy, Romeo and Juliet, Antony and Cleopatra, Arthur and Guinevere, Tristan and Isolde. From ancient fables to the latest blockbuster, the theme of a strong man coming to rescue a beautiful woman is universal to human nature. It is written in our hearts, one of the core desires of every man and every woman.

I met Stasi in high school, but it wasn't until late in college that our romance began. Up till that point we were simply friends. When one of us came home for the weekend, we'd give the other a call just to "hang out" — see a movie, go to a party. Then one summer night something shifted. I dropped by to see Stasi; she came sauntering down the hall barefoot, wearing a pair of blue jeans and a white blouse with lace around the collar and the top buttons undone. The sun had lightened her hair and darkened her skin and how is it I never realized she was the beautiful maiden before? We kissed that night, and though I'd kissed a few girls in my time I had never tasted a kiss like that. Needless to say, I was history. Our friendship had turned to love without my really knowing how or why, only that I wanted to be with this woman for the rest of my life. As far as Stasi was concerned, I was her knight.

Why is it that ten years later I wondered if I even wanted to be married to her anymore? Divorce was looking like a pretty decent option for the both of us. So many couples wake one day to find they no longer love each other. Why do most of us get lost somewhere between "once upon a time" and "happily ever after"? Most passionate romances seem to end with evenings in front of the TV. Why does the dream seem so unattainable, fading from view even as we discover it for ourselves? Our culture has grown cynical about the fable. Don Henley says, "We've been poisoned by these fairy tales." There are dozens of books out to refute the myth, books like *Beyond Cinderella* and *The Death of Cinderella*.

No, we have not been poisoned by fairy tales and they are not merely "myths." Far from it. The truth is, we have not taken them seriously enough. As Roland Hein says, "Myths are stories which confront us with something transcendent and eternal." In the case of our fair maiden, we have overlooked two very crucial aspects to that myth. On the one hand, none of us ever really believed the sorcerer was real. We thought we could have the maiden without a fight. Honestly, most of us guys thought our biggest battle was asking her out. And second, we have not understood the tower and its relation to her wound; the damsel is in distress. If masculinity has come under assault, femininity has been brutalized. Eve is the crown of creation, remember? She embodies the exquisite beauty and the exotic mystery of God in a way that nothing else in all creation even comes close to. And so she is the special target of the Evil One; he turns his most vicious malice against her. If he can destroy her or keep her captive, he can ruin the story.

EVE'S WOUND

Every woman can tell you about her wound; some came with violence, others came with neglect. Just as every little boy is asking one question, every little girl is, as well. But her question isn't so much about her strength. No, the deep cry of a little girl's heart is *am I lovely?* Every woman needs to know that she is exquisite and exotic and *chosen*. This is core to her identity, the way she bears the

278

image of God. *Will you pursue me? Do you delight in me? Will you fight for me?* And like every little boy, she has taken a wound as well. The wound strikes right at the core of her heart of beauty and leaves a devastating message with it: *No. You're not beautiful and no one will really fight for you.* Like your wound, hers almost always comes at the hand of her father.

A little girl looks to her father to know if she is lovely. The power he has to cripple or to bless is just as significant to her as it is to his son. If he's a violent man he may defile her verbally or sexually. The stories I've heard from women who have been abused would tear your heart out. Janet was molested by her father when she was three; around the age of seven he showed her brothers how to do it. The assault continued until she moved away to college. What is a violated woman to think about her beauty? Am I lovely? The message is, *No . . . you are dirty. Anything attractive about you is dark and evil.* The assault continues as she grows up, through violent men and passive men. She may be stalked; she may be ignored. Either way, her heart is violated and the message is driven farther in: *you are not desired, you will not be protected, no one will fight for you.* The tower is built brick by brick, and when she's a grown woman it can be a fortress.

If her father is passive, a little girl will suffer a silent abandonment. Stasi remembers playing hide-and-seek in her house as a girl of five or six. She'd find a perfect place to crawl into, full of excited anticipation of the coming pursuit. Snuggled up in a closet, she would wait for someone to find her. No one ever did; not even after she was missing for an hour. That picture became the defining image of her life. No one noticed; no one pursued. The youngest in her family, Stasi just seemed to get lost in the shuffle. Her dad traveled a lot, and when he was home he spent most of his time in front of the TV. An older brother and sister were trouble in their teens; Stasi got the message, "Just don't be a problem; we've already got too much to handle." So she hid some more — hid her desires, hid her dreams, hid her heart. Sometimes she would pretend to be sick just to get a drop or two of attention.

Like so many unloved young women, Stasi turned to boys to try to hear what she never heard from her father. Her high school boyfriend betrayed her on prom night, told her he had been using her, that he really loved someone else. The man she dated in college became verbally abusive.

But when a woman never hears she's worth fighting for, she comes to believe that's the sort of treatment she deserves. It's a form of attention, in a twisted way; maybe it's better than nothing. Then we fell in love on that magical summer night. But Stasi married a frightened, driven man who had an affair with his work because he wouldn't risk engaging a woman he sensed he wasn't enough for. I wasn't mean; I wasn't evil. I was nice. And let me tell you, a hesitant man is the last thing in the world a woman needs. She needs a lover and a warrior, not a Really Nice Guy. Her worst fear was realized — I will never really be loved, never really be fought for. And so she hid some more.

Years into our marriage I found myself blindsided by it all. Where is the beauty I once saw? What happened to the woman I fell in love with? I didn't really expect an answer to my question; it was more a shout of rage than a desperate plea. But Jesus answered me anyway. *She's still in there, but she's captive. Are you willing to go in after her?* I realized that I had — like so many men — married for safety. I married a woman I thought would never challenge me as a man. Stasi adored me; what more did I need to do? I wanted to look like the knight, but I didn't want to bleed like one. I was deeply

mistaken about the whole arrangement. I
didn't know about the tower, or the dragon,
or what my strength was for. The number
one problem between men and their women
is that we men, when asked to truly fight for
her . . . hesitate. We are still seeking to save
ourselves; we have forgotten the deep pleasure of spilling our life for another.

OFFERING OUR STRENGTH

> There are three things that are too
>   amazing for me,
> four that I do not understand:
> the way of an eagle in the sky,
> the way of a snake on a rock,
> the way of a ship on the high seas,
> and the way of a man with a maiden.
>   (Prov. 30:18–19)

Agur son of Jakeh is onto something here.
There is something mythic in the way a man
is with a woman. Our sexuality offers a parable of amazing depth when it comes to being
masculine and feminine. The man comes to
offer his strength and the woman invites the
man into herself, an act that requires courage
and vulnerability and selflessness for both of
them. Notice first that if the man will not rise
to the occasion, nothing will happen. He

282

must move; his strength must swell before he can enter her. But neither will the love consummate unless the woman opens herself in stunning vulnerability. When both are living as they were meant to live, the man enters his woman and offers her his strength. He *spills himself there,* in her, for her; she draws him in, embraces and envelops him. When all is over he is spent; but ah, what a sweet death it is.

And that is how life is created. The beauty of a woman arouses a man to play the man; the strength of a man, offered tenderly to his woman, allows her to be beautiful; it brings life to her and to many. This is far, far more than sex and orgasm. It is a reality that extends to every aspect of our lives. When a man withholds himself from his woman, he leaves her without the life only he can bring. This is never more true than how a man offers — or does not offer — his words. Life and death are in the power of the tongue says Proverbs (18:21). She is made for and craves words from him. I just went upstairs to get a glass of water from the kitchen; Stasi was in there baking Christmas cookies. The place was a mess; to be honest, so was she, covered with flour and wearing a pair of old slippers. But there was something in her eye, something soft and tender, and I said to her, "You look pretty." The tension in her shoulders gave way; something twinkled in her spirit; she sighed and smiled. "Thank you," she said, almost shyly.

If the man refuses to offer himself, then his wife will remain empty and barren. A violent man destroys with his words; a silent man starves his wife. "She's wilting," a friend confessed to me about his new bride. "If she's wilting then you're withholding something," I said. Actually, it was several things — his words, his touch, but mostly his *delight*. There are so many other ways this plays out in life. A man who leaves his wife with the children and the bills to go and find another, easier life has denied them his strength. He has sacrificed them when he should have sacrificed his strength *for* them. What makes Maximus or William Wallace so heroic is simply this: They are willing to die to set others free.

This sort of heroism is what we see in the life of Joseph, the husband of Mary and the stepfather to Jesus Christ. I don't think we've fully appreciated what he did for them. Mary, an engaged young woman, almost a girl, turns up pregnant with a pretty wild story: "I'm carrying God's child." The situation is scandalous. What is Joseph to think; what is he to feel? Hurt, confused, betrayed no doubt. But he's a good man; he will not have her stoned, he will simply "divorce her quietly" (Matt. 1:19).

An angel comes to him in a dream (which shows you what it sometimes takes to get a good man to do the right thing) to convince him that Mary is telling the truth and he is to follow through with the marriage. This is going to cost him. Do you know what he's going to endure if he marries a woman the whole community thinks is an adulteress? He will be shunned by his business associates and most of his clients; he will certainly lose his standing in society and perhaps even his place in the synagogue. To see the pain he's in for, notice the insult that crowds will later use against Jesus. "Isn't this Joseph and Mary's son?" they say with a sneer and a nudge and a wink. In other words, we know who you are — the bastard child of that slut and her foolish carpenter. Joseph will pay big-time for this move. Does he withhold? No, he offers Mary his strength; he steps right between her and all of that mess and takes it on the chin. He spends himself for her.

"They will be called oaks of righteousness" (Isa. 61:3). There, under the shadow of a man's strength, a woman finds rest.

The masculine journey takes a man away from the woman *so that he might return to her.* He goes to find his strength; he returns to offer it. He tears down the walls of the tower that has held her with his words and with his actions. He speaks to her heart's deepest question in a thousand ways. *Yes, you are lovely. Yes, there is one who will fight for you.* But because most men have not yet fought the battle, most women are still in the tower.

USING HER

Most men want the maiden without any sort of cost to themselves. They want all the joys of the beauty without any of the woes of the battle. This is the sinister nature of pornography — enjoying the woman at her expense. Pornography is what happens when a man insists on being energized by a woman; he *uses* her to get a feeling that he is a man. It is a false strength, as I've said, because it depends on an outside source rather than emanating from deep within his center. And it is the paragon of selfishness. He offers nothing and takes everything. We are warned about this sort of man in the story of Judah and Tamar, a story that if it weren't in the Bible you would have thought I drew straight from a television miniseries.

Judah is the fourth son born to Jacob. You might remember him as the one who came up with the idea to sell his brother Joseph into slavery. Judah has three sons himself. When the eldest becomes a man, Judah finds a wife for him named Tamar. For reasons not fully explained to us, their marriage is short-lived. "But Er, Judah's firstborn, was wicked in the LORD's sight; so the LORD put him to death" (Gen. 38:7). Judah gives his second son to Tamar, as was the law and custom of that time. It is Onan's responsibility to raise up children in his brother's name; but he refuses to do it. He is a proud and self-centered man who angers the Lord, "so he put him to death also" (38:10). You're beginning to get the idea here: selfish men, a woman wronged, and the Lord is mad.

Judah has one son left — Shelah. The boy is the last of his strength and Judah has no intention of spending it on Tamar's behalf. He lies to Tamar, telling her to go back home and when Shelah is old enough he'll give him to her as her husband. He does not. What follows is hard to believe, especially when you consider that Tamar is a righteous woman. She disguises herself as a prostitute and sits by the road Judah is known to use. He has sex with her (uses her), but is unable to pay. Tamar takes his seal and cord and staff as a pledge. Later, word gets out that Tamar is pregnant; Judah is filled with what he insists is righteous indignation. He demands that she be burned to death, at which point Tamar produces the witness against him. "See if you recognize whose seal and cord and staff these are." Judah is nailed. He more than recognizes them — he realizes what he's been doing all along. "She is more righteous than I, since I wouldn't give her to my son Shelah" (38:25–26).

A sobering story of what happens when men selfishly refuse to spend their strength on behalf of the woman. But the same thing happens in all sorts of other ways. Pretty women endure this abuse all the time. They are pursued, but not really; they are wanted, but only superficially. They learn to offer their bodies but never, ever their souls. Most men, you see, marry for safety; they choose a woman who will make them feel like a man but never really challenge them to be one. A young man whom I admire is wrestling between the woman he is dating and one he knew but could not capture years ago. Rachel, the woman he is currently dating, is asking a lot of him; truth be told, he feels in way over his head. Julie, the woman he did not pursue, seems more idyllic; in his imagination she would be the perfect mate. Life with Rachel is tumultuous; life with Julie seems calm and tranquil. "You want the Bahamas," I said. "Rachel is the North Atlantic. Which one requires a true man?" In a brilliant twist of plot, God turns our scheme for safety on us, requiring us to play the man.

Why don't men offer what they have to their women? Because we know down in our guts that it won't be enough. There is an emptiness to Eve after the Fall, and no matter how much you pour into her she will never be filled. This is where so many men falter. Either they refuse to give what they can, or they keep pouring and pouring into her and all the while feel like a failure because she is still needing more. "There are three things that are never satisfied," warns Agur son of Jakeh, "four things that never say, 'Enough!': the grave, the barren womb, land, which is never satisfied with water, and fire, which never says, 'Enough!' " The barrenness of Eve you can never hope to fill. She needs God more than she needs you, just as you need him more than you need her.

So what do you do? Offer what you have.

"I'm afraid it won't work," a client said to me when I suggested he move back toward his wife. "She's given up on me coming through for her," he confessed, "and that's good." "No it's not," I said. "That's awful." He was headed to a family reunion back east and I suggested he bring his wife with him, make it a vacation for the two of them. "You need to move toward her." "What if it doesn't work?" he asked. So many men are asking the same question. Work for what? Validate you as a man? Resurrect her heart in a day? Do you see now that you can't bring your question to Eve? No matter how good a man you are you can never be enough. If she's the report card on your strength then you'll ultimately get an F. But that's not why you love her — to get a good grade. You love her because that's what you are made to do; that's what a real man does.

EVE TO ADAM

My friend Jan says that a woman who is living out her true design will be "valiant, vulnerable, and scandalous." That's a far cry from the "church ladies" we hold up as models of Christian femininity, those busy and tired and rigid women who have reduced their hearts to a few mild desires and pretend everything is going just great. Compare their femininity with that of the women named in the genealogy of Jesus. In a list that is nearly all men, Matthew mentions four women: Tamar, Rahab, Ruth, and "Uriah's wife" (1:3, 5–6). That Bathsheba goes unnamed tells you of God's disappointment with her, and of his delight in these three whom he takes a notable exception to name in an otherwise all-male cast. Tamar, Rahab and Ruth . . . whoa; this will open up new horizons of "biblical femininity" for you.

Tamar we now know. Rahab is in the "hall of fame of faith" in Hebrews 11 for committing treason. That's right — she hid the spies who were coming in to scope out Jericho before battle. I've never heard a woman's group study Tamar or Rahab. But what about Ruth? She's often held up as a model at women's studies and retreats — but not in the way God holds her up. The book of Ruth is devoted to one question: How does a good woman help her man to play the man? The answer: She seduces him. She uses all she has as a woman to arouse him to be a man. Ruth, as you'll remember, is the daughter-in-law of a Jewish woman named Naomi. Both women have lost their husbands and are in a pretty bad way; they have no man looking out for

291

them, their financial status is below the poverty line, and they are vulnerable in many other ways as well. Things begin to look up when Ruth catches the eye of a wealthy single man named Boaz. Boaz is a good man, this we know. He offers her some protection and some food. But Boaz is not giving Ruth what she really needs — a ring.

So what does Ruth do? She seduces him. Here's the scene: The men have been working dawn till dusk to bring in the barley harvest; they've just finished and now it's party time. Ruth takes a bubble bath and puts on a knockout dress; then she waits for the right moment. That moment happens to be late in the evening after Boaz has had a little too much to drink: "When Boaz had finished eating and drinking and was in good spirits . . ." (Ruth 3:7). "Good spirits" is in there for the more conservative readers. The man is drunk, which is evident from what he does next: pass out. ". . . He went over to lie down at the far end of the grain pile" (3:7). What happens next is simply scandalous; the verse continues, "Ruth approached quietly, uncovered his feet and lay down."

There is no possible reading of this passage that is "safe" or "nice." This is seduction pure and simple — and God holds it up for all women to follow when he not only gives Ruth her own book in the Bible but also names her in the genealogy. Yes, there are folks that'll try to tell you that it's perfectly common for a beautiful single woman "in that culture" to approach a single man (who's had too much to drink) in the middle of the night with no one else around (the far side of the grain pile) and tuck herself under the covers. They're the same folks who'll tell you that the Song of Solomon is nothing more than a "theological metaphor referring to Christ and his bride." Ask 'em what they do with passages like "Your stature is like that of the palm, and your breasts like clusters of fruit. I said 'I will climb the palm tree; I will take hold of its fruit' " (Song 7:7–8). That's a Bible study, right?

No, I do not think Ruth and Boaz had sex that night; I do not think anything inappropriate happened at all. But this is no fellowship potluck, either. I'm telling you that the church has really crippled women when it tells them that their beauty is vain and they are at their feminine best when they are "serving others." A woman is at her best when she is being a woman. Boaz needs a little help getting going and Ruth has some options. She can badger him: *All you do is work, work, work. Why won't you stand up*

293

and be a man? She can whine about it: *Boaz, pleeease hurry up and marry me.* She can emasculate him: *I thought you were a real man; I guess I was wrong.* Or she can use all she is as a woman to get him to use all he's got as a man. She can arouse, inspire, energize . . . seduce him. Ask your man what he'd prefer.

IT IS A BATTLE

Will you fight for her? That's the question Jesus asked me many years ago, right before our tenth anniversary, right at the time I was wondering what had happened to the woman I married. *You're on the fence, John,* he said. *Get in or get out.* I knew what he was saying — stop being a nice guy and act like a warrior. Play the man. I brought flowers, took her to dinner, and began to move back toward her in my heart. But I knew there was more. That night, before we went to bed, I prayed for Stasi in a way I'd never prayed for her before. Out loud, before all the heavenly hosts, I stepped between her and the forces of darkness that had been coming against her. Honestly, I didn't really know what I was doing, only that I needed to take on the dragon. All hell broke loose. Everything we've learned about spiritual warfare began that night. And

294

you know what happened? Stasi got free; the tower of her depression gave way as I began to truly fight for her.

And it's not just once, but again and again over time. That's where the myth really stumps us. Some men are willing to go in once, twice, even three times. But a warrior is in this for good. Oswald Chambers asks, "God spilt the life of his son that the world might be saved; are we prepared to spill out our lives?" Daniel is in the midst of a very hard, very unpromising battle for his wife. It's been years now without much progress and without much hope. Sitting in a restaurant the other night, tears in his eyes, this is what he said to me: "I'm not going anywhere. This is my place in the battle. This is the hill that I will die on." He has reached a point that we all must come to, sooner or later, when it's no longer about winning or losing. His wife may respond and she may not. That's really no longer the issue. The question is simply this: What kind of man do you want to be? Maximus? Wallace? Or Judah? A young pilot in the RAF wrote just before he went down in 1940, "The universe is so vast and so ageless that the life of one man can only be justified by the measure of his sacrifice."

As I write this chapter, Stasi and I have

just returned from a friend's wedding. It was the best nuptials either of us have ever been to; a wonderful, romantic, holy affair. The groom was young and strong and valiant; the bride was seductively beautiful. Which is what made it so excruciating for me. Oh to start over again, to do it all over the right way, marry as a young man knowing what I know now. I could have loved Stasi so much better; she could have loved me so much better as well. We've learned every lesson the hard way over our eighteen years. Any wisdom contained in these pages was paid for . . . dearly. On top of that Stasi and I were in a difficult place over the weekend; that was the campfire. Satan saw his opportunity and turned it into a bonfire *without even one word between us*. By the time we got to the reception, I didn't want to dance with her. I didn't even want to be in the same room. All the hurt and disappointment of the years — hers and mine — seemed to be the only thing that was ever true about our marriage.

It wasn't until later that I heard Stasi's side of the script, but here is how the two fit together. Stasi: *He's disappointed in me. No wonder why. Look at all these beautiful women. I feel fat and ugly.* Me: *I'm so tired of battling for our marriage. How I wish we could start over. It wouldn't be that hard, you know. There are other options. Look at all these beautiful women.* On and on it came, like a wave overwhelming the shore. Sitting at the table with a group of our friends, I felt I was going to suffocate; I had to get out of there, get some fresh air. Truth be told, when I left the reception I had no intention of going back. Either I'd wind up in a bar somewhere or back in our room watching TV. Thankfully, I found a small library off to the side of the reception hall; alone in that sanctuary I wrestled with all I was feeling for what seemed like an hour. (It was probably twenty minutes.) I grabbed a book but could not read; I tried to pray but did not want to. Finally, some words began to arise from my heart:

Jesus, come and rescue me. I know what's going on, I know this is assault. But right now it all feels so true. Jesus, deliver me. Get me out from under this waterfall. Speak to me, rescue my heart before I do something stupid. Deliver me, Lord.

Slowly, almost imperceptibly, the wave began to lift. My thoughts and emotions quieted down to a more normal size. Clarity was returning. The campfire was just a campfire again. *Jesus, you know the pain and disappointment in my heart. What would you have me do?* (The bar was no longer an option, but I was still planning to just go straight to my room for the rest of the night.) *I want you to go back in there and ask your wife to dance.* I knew he was right; I knew that somewhere down deep inside that's what my true heart would want to do. But the desire still seemed so far away. I lingered for five more minutes, hoping he had another option for me. He remained silent, but the assault was over and the bonfire was only embers. Once more I knew the man I wanted to be.

I went back to the reception and asked Stasi to dance; for the next two hours we had one of the best evenings we've had in a long time. We nearly lost to the Evil One; instead, it will go down as a memory we'll share with our friends for a long, long time.

CLOSE

Stasi has given me a number of wonderful presents over the years, but last Christmas was unforgettable. We'd finished with the feeding frenzy the boys call unwrapping presents. Stasi slipped out of the room with the words, "Close your eyes . . . I have a surprise for you." After a good deal of rustling and whispers, she told me I could look. Before me was a long rectangular box on the family room floor. "Open it," she said. I removed the bow and lifted the lid. Inside was a full-size claymore, a Scottish broadsword exactly like the one used by William Wallace. I had been looking for one for several months, but Stasi did not know that. It was not on my Christmas list. She had done this out of the vision of her own heart, as a way of thanking me for fighting for her.

Here is what her note read:

Because you are a Braveheart, fighting for the hearts of so many people . . . and especially for mine. Thanks to you I know a freedom I never thought was possible. Merry Christmas.

Chapter Eleven

AN ADVENTURE
TO LIVE

Dark and cold we may be, but this
Is no winter now. The frozen misery
Of centuries breaks, cracks, begins to move;
The thunder is the thunder of the floes,
The thaw, the flood, the upstart Spring
Thank God our time is now when wrong
Comes up to face us everywhere,
Never to leave us till we take
The longest stride of soul men ever took.
— CHRISTOPHER FRY

The place where God calls you is the place where
your deep gladness and the world's deep hunger
meet.
— FREDERICK BUECHNER

There is a river that winds its way through southern Oregon, running down from the Cascades to the coast, which has also wound its way through my childhood, carving a path in the canyons of my memory. As a young boy I spent many summer days on the Rogue, fishing and swimming and picking blackberries; but mostly, fishing. I loved the name given to the river by French trappers; the river Scoundrel. It gave a mischievous benediction to my adventures there — I was a rogue on the Rogue. Those golden days of boyhood are some of my most cherished memories and so last summer I took Stasi and the boys there, to share with them a river and a season from my life. The lower part of the Rogue runs through some hot and dry country in the summer months, especially in late July, and we were looking forward to kayaking as an excuse to get really wet and find a little adventure of our own.

There is a rock that juts out over that river somewhere between Morrison's Lodge and the Foster Bar. The canyon narrows there and the Rogue deepens and pauses for a moment in its rush to the sea. High rock walls rise on either side, and on the north — the side only boaters can reach — is Jumping Rock. Cliff jumping is one of our family favorites, especially when it's hot and dry and the jump is high enough so that it takes your breath away as you plunge beneath the warmer water at the top, down to where it's dark and cold, so cold that it sends you gasping back for the surface and the sun. Jumping Rock is perched above the river at about the height of a two-story house plus some, tall enough that you can slowly count to five before you hit the water (it's barely a two count from the high dive at your local pool). There's a faculty built into the human brain that makes every cliff seem twice the height when you're looking down from the top and everything in you says, *Don't even think about it.*

So you don't think about it, you just hurl yourself off out into the middle of the canyon, and then you free-fall for what feels like enough time to recite the Gettysburg Address and all your senses are on maximum alert as you plunge into the cold water. When you come back up the crowd is cheering and something in you is also cheering because *you did it.* We all jumped that day, first me, then Stasi, Blaine, Sam, and even Luke. Then some big hulking guy who was going to back down once he saw what the view was like from above, but he had to jump because Luke did it and he couldn't live with himself knowing he'd cowered while a six-year-old boy hurled himself off. After that first jump you have to do it again, partly because you can't believe you did it and partly because the fear has given way to the thrill of such freedom. We let the sun heat us up again and then . . . bombs away.

I want to live my whole life like that. I want to love with much more abandon and stop waiting for others to love me first. I want to hurl myself into a creative work worthy of God. I want to charge the fields at Banockburn, follow Peter as he followed Christ out onto the sea, pray from my heart's true *desire*. As the poet George Chapman has said,

> Give me a spirit that on this life's
> rough sea
> Loves to have his sails fill'd with a
> lusty wind
> Even till his sail-yards tremble, his
> masts crack,
> And his rapt ship runs on her side so
> low
> That she drinks water, and her keel
> ploughs air.

Life is not a problem to be solved; it is an adventure to be lived. That's the nature of it and has been since the beginning when God set the dangerous stage for this high-stakes drama and called the whole wild enterprise *good*. He rigged the world in such a way that it only works when we embrace *risk* as the theme of our lives, which is to say, only when we live by faith. A man just won't be happy until he's got adventure in his work, in his love and in his spiritual life.

ASKING THE RIGHT QUESTION

Several years ago I was thumbing through the introduction of a book when I ran across a sentence that changed my life. God is intimately personal with us and he speaks in ways that are peculiar to our own quirky hearts — not just through the Bible, but through the whole of creation. To Stasi he speaks through movies. To Craig he speaks through rock and roll (he called me the other day after listening to "Running Through the Jungle" to say he was fired up to go study the Bible). God's word to me comes in many ways — through sunsets and friends and films and music and wilderness and books. But he's got an especially humorous thing going with me and books. I'll be browsing through a secondhand book shop when out of a thousand volumes one will say, "Pick me up" — just like Augustine in his *Confessions*. *Tolle legge* — take up and read. Like a master fly fisherman God cast his fly to this cruising trout. In the introduction to the book that I rose to this day, the author (Gil Bailie) shares a piece of advice given to him some years back by a spiritual mentor:

Don't ask yourself what the world needs. Ask yourself what makes you come alive, and go do that, because what the world needs is people who have come alive.

I was struck dumb. It could have been Balaam's donkey, for all I was concerned. Suddenly my life up till that point made sense in a sickening sort of way; I realized I was living a script written for me by someone else. All my life I had been asking the world to tell me what to do with myself. This is different from seeking counsel or advice; what I wanted was freedom from responsibility and especially freedom from risk. I wanted someone else to tell me who to be. Thank God it didn't work. The scripts they handed me I simply could not bring myself to play for very long. Like Saul's armor, they never fit. Can a world of posers tell you to do anything but pose yourself? As Buechner says, we are in constant danger of being not actors in the drama of our lives but reactors, "to go where the world takes us, to drift with whatever current happens to be running the strongest." Reading the counsel given to Bailie I knew it was God speaking to me. It was an invitation to come out of Ur. I set the volume down without turning another page and walked out of that bookstore to find a life worth living.

I applied to graduate school and got accepted. That program would turn out to be far more than a career move; out of the transformation that took place there I became a writer, counselor, and speaker. The whole trajectory of my life changed and with it the lives of many, many other people. But I almost didn't go. You see, when I applied to school I hadn't a nickel to pay for it. I was married with three children and a mortgage, and that's the season when most men completely abandon their dreams and back down from jumping off anything. The risk just seems too great. On top of it all, I received a call about that time from a firm back in Washington, D.C., offering me a plum job at an incredible salary. I would be in a prestigious company, flying in some very powerful circles, making great money. God was thickening the plot, testing my resolve. Down one road was my dream and desire, which I had no means to pay for, and an absolutely uncertain future after that; down the other was a comfortable step up the ladder of success, a very obvious next career move and the total loss of my soul.

I went to the mountains for the weekend to sort things out. Life makes more sense standing alone by a lake at high elevation with a fly rod in hand. The tentacles of the world and my false self seemed to give way as I climbed up into the Holy Cross Wilderness. On the second day God began to speak. *John, you can take that job if you want to. It's not a sin. But it'll kill you and you know it.* He was right; it had False Self written all over it. *If you want to follow Me,* he continued, *I'm heading that way.* I knew exactly what he meant — "that way" headed into wilderness, frontier. The following week three phone calls came in amazing succession. The first was from the Washington firm; I told them I was not their man, to call somebody else. As I hung up the phone my false self was screaming *what are you doing?!* The next day the phone rang again; it was my wife, telling me that the university had called wanting to know where my first tuition installment was. On the third day a call came from a longtime friend who had been praying for me and my decision. "We think you ought to go to school," he said. "And we want to pay your way."

> Two roads diverged in a wood and I,
> I took the one less traveled by.
> And that has made all the difference.

WHAT ARE YOU WAITING FOR?

Where would we be today if Abraham had carefully weighed the pros and cons of God's invitation and decided that he'd rather hang on to his medical benefits, three weeks paid vacation and retirement plan in Ur? What would have happened if Moses had listened to his mother's advice to "never play with matches" and lived a careful, cautious life steering clear of all burning bushes? You wouldn't have the gospel if Paul had concluded that the life of a Pharisee, while not everything a man dreams for, was at least predictable and certainly more stable than following a voice he heard on the Damascus road. After all, people hear voices all the time and who really knows whether it's God or just one's imagination. Where would we be if Jesus was not fierce and wild and romantic to the core? Come to think of it, we wouldn't *be* at all if God hadn't taken that enormous risk of us in the first place.

Most men spend the energy of their lives trying to eliminate risk, or squeezing it down to a more manageable size. Their children hear "no" far more than they hear "yes"; their employees feel chained up and their wives are equally bound. If it works, if a man succeeds in securing his life against all risk, he'll wind up in a cocoon of self-protection and wonder all the while why he's suffocating. If it doesn't work, he curses God, redoubles his efforts and his blood pressure. When you look at the structure of the false self men tend to create, it always revolves around two themes: seizing upon some sort of competence and rejecting anything that cannot be controlled. As David Whyte says, "The price of our vitality is the sum of all our fears."

For murdering his brother, God sentences Cain to the life of a restless wanderer; five verses later Cain is building a city (Gen. 4:12, 17). That sort of commitment — the refusal to trust God and the reach for control — runs deep in every man. Whyte talks about the difference between the false self's desire "to have power *over* experience, to control all events and consequences, and the soul's wish to have power *through* experience, *no matter what that may be.*" You literally sacrifice your soul and your true power when you insist on controlling things, like the guy Jesus talked about who thought he finally pulled it all off, built himself some really nice barns and died the same night. "What will it profit a man if he gains the whole world, and loses his own soul?" (Mark 8:36 NKJV). You can lose your soul, by the way, long before you die.

Canadian biologist Farley Mowat had a dream of studying wolves in their native habitat, out in the wilds of Alaska. The book *Never Cry Wolf* is based on that lonely research expedition. In the film version Mowat's character is a bookworm named Tyler who has never so much as been camping. He hires a crazy old Alaskan bush pilot named Rosie Little to get him and all his equipment into the remote Blackstone Valley in the dead of winter. Flying in Little's single-engine Cessna over some of the most beautiful, rugged, and dangerous wilderness in the world, Little pries Tyler for the secret to his mission:

LITTLE: Tell me, Tyler . . . what's in the valley of the Blackstone? What is it? Manganese? (Silence) Can't be oil. Is it gold?

310

TYLER: It's kind of hard to say.

LITTLE: You're a smart man, Tyler
. . . you keep your own
counsel. We're all of us
prospectors up here, right,
Tyler? Scratchin' for that
. . . that one crack in the
ground . . . and never have
to scratch again.
(After a pause)
I'll let you in on a little
secret, Tyler. The gold's
not in the ground. The gold
is not anywhere up here.
The real gold is south at 60,
sittin' in living rooms,
facing the boob tube bored
to death. Bored to death,
Tyler.

Suddenly the plane's engine coughs a few times, sputters, gasps . . . and then simply cuts out. The only sound is the wind over the wings.

LITTLE: (Groans) Oh, Lord.

TYLER: (Panicked) What's wrong?

LITTLE: Take the stick.

Little hands over control of the powerless

plane to Tyler (who has never flown a plane in his life) and starts frantically rummaging around in an old toolbox between the seats. Unable to find what he's looking for, Little explodes. Screaming, he empties the toolbox all over the plane. Then just as abruptly he stops, calmly rubbing his face with his hands.

TYLER: (Still panicked and trying to fly the plane) What's wrong?

LITTLE: Boredom, Tyler. Boredom . . . that's what's wrong. How do you beat boredom, Tyler? Adventure. ADVENTURE, Tyler!

Little then kicks the door of the plane open and nearly disappears outside, banging on something — a frozen fuel line perhaps. The engine kicks back in just as they are about to fly into the side of a mountain. Little grabs the stick and pulls them into a steep ascent, barely missing the ridge and then easing off into a long, majestic valley below.

Rosie Little may be a madman, but he's also a genius. He knows the secret to a man's heart, the cure for what ails him. Too many men forsake their dreams because they aren't willing to risk, or fear they aren't up to the challenge, or are never told that those desires deep in their heart are *good*. But the soul of a man, the real gold Little refers to, isn't made for controlling things; he's made for adventure. Something in us remembers, however faintly, that when God set man on the earth he gave us an incredible mission — a charter to explore, build, conquer, and care for all creation. It was a blank page waiting to be written; a clean canvas waiting to be painted. Well, sir, God never revoked that charter. It's still there, waiting for a man to seize it.

If you had permission to do what you really want to do, what would you do? Don't ask *how*, that will cut your desire off at the knees. *How* is never the right question; *how* is a faithless question. It means "unless I can see my way clearly I won't believe it, won't venture forth." When the angel told Zechariah that his ancient wife would bear him a son named John, Zechariah asked how and was struck dumb for it. *How* is God's department. He is asking you *what*. What is written in your heart? What makes you come alive? If you could do what you've always wanted to do, what would it be? You see, a man's calling is written on his true heart, and he discovers it when he enters the frontier of his deep desires. To paraphrase Bailie, don't ask yourself what the world needs, ask yourself what makes you come alive because what the world needs are *men* who have come alive.

The invitation in the book shop, I must note, was given to me some years into my Christian life when the transformation of my character was at a point that I could hear it without running off and doing something stupid. I've met men who've used advice like it as permission to leave their wife and run off with their secretary. They are *deceived* about what it is they really want, what they are made for. There is a design God has woven into the fabric of this world, and if we violate it we cannot hope to find life. Because our hearts have strayed so far from home, he's given us the Law as a sort of handrail to help us back from the precipice. But the goal of Christian discipleship is the transformed heart; we move from a boy who needs the Law to the man who is able to live by the Spirit of the law. "My counsel is this: Live freely, animated and motivated by God's Spirit. Then you won't feed the compulsions of selfishness . . . Legalism is helpless in bringing this about; it only gets in the way" (Gal. 5:16, 23 *The Message*).

A man's life becomes an adventure, the whole thing takes on a transcendent purpose when he releases control in exchange for the recovery of the dreams in his heart. Sometimes those dreams are buried deep and it takes some unearthing to get to them. We pay attention to our desire. Often the clues are in our past, in those moments when we found ourselves loving what we were doing. The details and circumstances change as we grow, but the themes remain the same. Dale was the neighborhood ring leader as a boy; in college, he was captain of the tennis team. What makes him come alive is when he is leading men. For Charles it was art; he was always drawing as a child. In high school, what he loved best was ceramics class. He gave up painting after college and finally came alive again when at age fifty-one he got it back.

To recover his heart's desire a man needs to get away from the noise and distraction of his daily life for time with his own soul. He needs to head into the wilderness, to silence and solitude. Alone with himself, he allows whatever is there to come to the surface. Sometimes it is grief for so much lost time. There, beneath the grief, are desires long forsaken. Sometimes it even starts with temptation, when a man thinks that what will really make him come alive is something unholy. At that point he should ask himself, "What is the desire *beneath* this desire? What is it I'm wanting that I think I'll find there?" However the desire begins to surface, we pick up that trail when we allow a cry to rise from the depths of our soul, a cry, as Whyte says, "for a kind of forgotten courage, one difficult to hear, demanding not a raise, but another life."

> I have studied many times
> The marble which was chiseled for
>   me —
> A boat with a furled sail at rest in a
>   harbor.
> In truth it pictures not my destination
> But my life.
> For love was offered me, and I shrank
>   from its disillusionment;
> Sorrow knocked at my door, but I
>   was afraid
> Ambition called to me, but I dreaded
>   the chances.
> Yet all the while I hungered for
>   meaning in my life
> And now I know that we must lift the
>   sail
> And catch the winds of destiny
> Wherever they drive the boat.

To put meaning in one's life may end
  in madness,
But life without meaning is the tor-
  ture
Of restlessness and vague desire —
  It is a boat longing for the sea and
  yet afraid.
(EDGAR LEE MASTERS)

INTO THE UNKNOWN

"The spiritual life cannot be made sub-urban," said Howard Macey. "It is always frontier and we who live in it must accept and even rejoice that it remains untamed." The greatest obstacle to realizing our dreams is the false self's hatred of mystery. That's a problem, you see, because *mystery is essential to adventure.* More than that, mystery is the heart of the universe and the God who made it. The most important aspects of any man's world — his relationship with his God and with the people in his life, his calling, the spiritual battles he'll face — every one of them is fraught with mystery. But that is not a bad thing; it is a joyful, rich part of reality and essential to our soul's thirst for adven-ture. As Oswald Chambers says,

Naturally, we are inclined to be so mathematical and calculating that we look upon uncertainty as a bad thing . . . Certainty is the mark of the common-sense life; gracious uncertainty is the mark of the spiritual life. To be certain of God means that we are uncertain in all our ways, we do not know what a day may bring forth. This is generally said with a sigh of sadness; it should rather be an expression of breathless expectation. (*My Utmost for His Highest*)

There are no formulas with God. Period. So there are no formulas for the man who follows him. God is a Person, not a doctrine. He operates not like a system — not even a theological system — but with all the originality of a truly free and alive person. "The realm of God is dangerous," says Archbishop Anthony Bloom. "You must enter into it and not just seek information about it. Take Joshua and the Battle of Jericho. The Israelites are staged to make their first military strike into the promised land and there's a lot hanging on this moment — the morale of the troops, their confidence in Joshua, not to mention their reputation that will precede them to every other enemy that awaits. This is their D-Day, so to speak, and word is going to get around. How does God get the whole thing off to a good start? He has them march around the city blowing trumpets for a week; on the seventh day he has them do it seven times and then give a big holler. It works marvelously, of course. And you know what? It never happens again. Israel never uses that tactic again.

There's Gideon and his army reduced from thirty-two thousand to three-hundred. What's their plan of attack? Torches and water pots. It also works splendidly and it also never happens again. You recall Jesus healing the blind — he never does it the same way twice. I hope you're getting the idea because the church has really been taken in by the world on this one. The Modern Era hated mystery; we desperately wanted a means of controlling our own lives and we seemed to find the ultimate Tower of Babel in the scientific method. Don't get me wrong — science has given us many wonderful advances in sanitation, medicine, transportation. But we've tried to use those methods to tame the wildness of the spiritual frontier. We take the latest marketing methods, the newest business management fad, and we apply it to ministry. The problem with modern Christianity's obsession with principles is that it removes any real conversation with God. Find the principle, apply the principle — what do you need God for? So Oswald Chambers warns us, "Never make a principle out of your experience; let God be as original with other people as he is with you.

Originality and creativity are essential to personhood and to masculine strength. The adventure begins and our *real* strength is released when we no longer rely on formulas. God is an immensely creative Person and he wants his sons to live that way too. There is a great picture of this in *Raiders of the Lost Ark,* of all places. Of course Indiana Jones is a swashbuckling hero who can handle ancient history, beautiful women, and a forty-five with ease. But the real test of the man comes when all his resources have failed. He's finally found the famous ark, but the Germans have stolen it from him and loaded it onto a truck. They're about to drive off with his dreams under heavy Nazi military protection. Jones and his two companions are watching helplessly as victory slips through their fingers. But Indiana is not finished; oh no, the game has just begun. He says to his friends:

JONES: Get back to Cairo. Get us some transport to England

	. . . boat, plane, anything. Meet me at Omars. Be ready for me. I'm going after that truck.
SAULACH:	How?
JONES:	I don't know I'm making this up as I go.

When it comes to living and loving, what's required is a willingness to jump in with both feet and be creative as you go. Here's but one example: A few years ago I got home from a trip on a Sunday afternoon and found the boys playing out on the front yard. It was a cold November day, too cold to be outside, and so I asked them what was up. "Mom kicked us out." Knowing there's often good reason when Stasi banishes them I pressed for a confession, but they maintained their innocence. So, I headed for the door to get the other side of the story. "I wouldn't go in there if I were you, Dad," Sam warned. "She's in a bad mood." I knew exactly what he was describing. The house was shut; inside all was dark and quiet.

Now, let me ask the men reading this: What was everything inside me telling me to do? *Run away. Don't even think about going in. Stay outside.* And you know what? I could have stayed outside and looked like a great dad, playing catch with my sons. But I am tired of being that man; I have run for years. Too many times I've played the coward and I'm sick of it. I opened the door, went inside, climbed the stairs, walked into our bedroom, sat down on the bed and asked my wife the most terrifying question any man ever asks his woman: "What's wrong?" After that it's all mystery. A woman doesn't want to be related to with formulas, and she certainly doesn't want to be treated like a project that has answers to it. She doesn't want to be solved; she wants to be *known*. Mason is absolutely right when he calls marriage the "Wild Frontier."

The same holds true for the spiritual battles that we face. After the Allies landed in France, they encountered something no one had planned or prepared them for: hedgerows. Enclosing every field from the sea to Verdun was a wall of earth, shrubs, and trees. Aerial photographs revealed the existence of the hedgerows, but the Allies assumed they were like the ones found across England, which are two feet high. The Norman hedgerows were ten feet high and impenetrable, a veritable fortress. If the Allies used the solitary gateways into each field, they were mowed down by German machine gunners. If they tried to drive their tanks up and over, the underbelly was exposed to antitank weapons. They had to improvise. American farmboys rigged all sorts of contraptions on the front of the Sherman tanks, which allowed them to punch holes for explosives or break right through the hedgerows. Grease monkeys from the states rebuilt damaged tanks over night. As one captain said,

> I began to realize something about the American Army I had never thought possible before. Although it is highly regimented and bureaucratic under garrison conditions, when the Army gets in the field, it relaxes and the individual initiative comes forward and does what has to be done. This type of flexibility was one of the great strengths of the American Army in World War II. (*Citizen Soldiers*)

It was truly Yankee ingenuity that won the war. This is where we are now — in the midst of battle without the training we really need, and there are few men around to show us how to do it. We are going to have to figure a lot of this out for ourselves. We know how to attend church; we've been taught not to swear or drink or smoke. We know how to be nice. But we don't really know how to fight, and we're going to have to learn as we go. That is where our strength will be crystallized, deepened, and *revealed*. A man is never more a man than when he embraces an adventure beyond his control, or when he walks into a battle he isn't sure of winning. As Antonio Machado wrote,

> Mankind owns four things
> That are no good at sea —
> Rudder, anchor, oars,
> And the fear of going down.

FROM FORMULA TO RELATIONSHIP

I'm not suggesting that the Christian life is chaotic or that a real man is flagrantly irresponsible. The poser who squanders his paycheck at the racetrack or the slot machines is not a man; he's a fool. The sluggard who quits his job and makes his wife go to work so he can stay home to practice his golf swing, thinking he'll make the pro tour, is "worse than an unbeliever" (1 Tim. 5:8). What I *am* saying is that our false self demands a formula before he'll engage; he wants a guarantee of success, and mister, you aren't going to get one. So there comes a time in a man's life when he's got to break away from all that and head off into the unknown with God. This is a vital part of our journey and if we balk here, the journey ends.

Before the moment of Adam's greatest trial God provided no step-by-step plan, gave no formula for how he was to handle the whole mess. That was not abandonment; that was the way God *honored* Adam. *You are a man, you don't need Me to hold you by the hand through this. You have what it takes.* What God *did* offer Adam was friendship. He wasn't left alone to face life; he walked with God in the cool of the day and there they talked about love and marriage and creativity, what lessons he was learning and what adventures were to come. This is what God is offering to us as well. As Chambers says,

There comes the baffling call of God in our lives also. The call of God can never be stated explicitly; it is implicit. The call of God is like the call of the sea, no one hears it but the one who has the nature of the sea in him. It cannot be stated definitely what the call of God is to, *because his call is to be in comradeship with himself* for his own purposes, and the test is to believe that God knows what he is after.

The only way to live in this adventure — with all its danger and unpredictability and immensely high stakes — is in an ongoing, intimate relationship with God. The control we so desperately crave is an illusion. Far better to give it up in exchange for God's offer of companionship, set aside stale formulas so that we might enter into an informal friendship. Abraham knew this; Moses did as well. Read through the first several chapters of Exodus — it's filled with a give-and-take between Moses and God. "Then the Lord said to Moses," "then Moses said to the Lord." The two act like they know each other, like they really are intimate allies. David — a man after God's own heart — also walked and warred and loved his way through life in a conversational intimacy with God.

When the Philistines heard that David had been anointed king over Israel, they went up in full force to search for him, but David heard about it and went down to the stronghold. Now the Philistines had come and spread out in the Valley of Rephaim; so David inquired of the

LORD, "Shall I go and attack the Philistines? Will you hand them over to me?" The LORD answered him, "Go, for I will surely hand the Philistines over to you." So David went to Baal Perazim, and there he defeated them . . . Once more the Philistines came up and spread out in the Valley of Rephaim; so David inquired of the LORD, and he answered, "Do not go straight up, but circle around behind them and attack them in front of the balsam trees. As soon as you hear the sound of marching in the tops of the balsam trees, move quickly, because that will mean the LORD has gone out in front of you to strike the Philistine army." So David did as the LORD commanded him, and he struck down the Philistines all the way from Gibeon to Gezer. (2 Sam. 5:17–20, 22–25)

Here again there is no rigid formula for David; it changes as he goes, relying on the counsel of God. This is the way every comrade and close companion of God lives. Jesus said, "I no longer call you servants, because a servant does not know his master's business. Instead, I have called you friends, for everything that I learned from my father I have made known to you" (John

15:15). God calls you his friend. He wants to talk to you — personally, frequently. As Dallas Willard writes, "The ideal for divine guidance is . . . a conversational relationship with God: the sort of relationship suited to friends who are mature personalities in a shared enterprise." Our whole journey into authentic masculinity centers around those cool-of-the-day talks with God. Simple questions change hassles to adventures; the events of our lives become opportunities for initiation. "What are you teaching me here, God? What are you asking me to do . . . or to let go of? What in my heart are you speaking to?"

FURTHER UP AND FURTHER IN

For years now I have wanted to climb one of the great peaks — Denali, perhaps, and after that maybe even Everest. Something calls to my heart every time I see a photo or read an account of another attempt. The allure of the wild places we have left haunts me, but there's also the desire for a challenge that requires everything I've got. Yes, even danger; maybe especially danger. Some people think I'm crazy, and I know that this dream may never be realized in my lifetime, but that does not discourage me; there is something symbolic about the desire and I cannot let it go. This is quite crucial for us to understand. We have desires in our hearts that are core to who and what we are; they are almost mythic in their meaning, waking in us something transcendent and eternal. But we can be mistaken about how those desires will be lived out. The way in which God fulfills a desire may be different from what first awakened it.

In the past year or so I've made a number of decisions that make no sense unless there is a God and I am his friend. I left my corporate job and struck out on my own, following a dream I've long feared. I've picked up the shattered pieces of a vision I lost when my best friend and partner Brent was killed in a climbing accident. What feels most crazy of all, I've opened my self to friendship again and a new partner, and we're heading out where Brent and I left off. The battle has been intense; a steep ascent that's taking everything I've got. The stakes I'm playing at now are immense — financially, sure, but more so spiritually, relationally. It's requiring a concentration of body, soul, and spirit I've never before endured.

What is perhaps the hardest part is the misunderstanding I live with from others on a daily basis. Sometimes the winds howl around me; other times I fear I'll fall. The other day I was feeling way out on the end of my rope, cutting a path across a sheer face of risk. Out of my heart rose a question. *What are we doing, God?*

We're climbing Everest.

Chapter Twelve

WRITING THE NEXT CHAPTER

I am sometimes almost terrified at the scope of the demands made upon me, at the perfection of the self-abandonment required of me; yet outside of such absoluteness can be no salvation.
— GEORGE MACDONALD

Freedom is useless if we don't exercise it as characters making choices . . . We are free to change the stories by which we live. Because we are genuine characters, and not mere puppets, we can choose our defining stories. We can do so because we actively participate in the creation of our stories. We are co-authors as well as characters. Few things are as encouraging as the realization that things can be different and that we have a role in making them so.
— DANIEL TAYLOR

Obey God in the thing he shows you, and in-

331

stantly the next thing is opened up. God will never reveal more truth about himself until you have obeyed what you know already . . . This chapter brings out the delight of real friendship with God.

— OSWALD CHAMBERS

At once they left their nets and followed him.
— MATTHEW 4:20

Now, reader, it is your turn to write — venture forth with God. Remember, don't ask yourself what the world needs . . .

ABOUT THE AUTHOR

John Eldredge is an author, counselor, and lecturer. For twelve years he was a writer and speaker for Focus on the Family, most recently serving on the faculty of the Focus on the Family Institute. Now John is director of Ransomed Heart™ Ministries, a teaching, counseling, and discipling fellowship devoted to helping people recover and live from their deep heart. John lives in Colorado Springs with his wife, Stasi, and their three sons. He loves living in Colorado so he can pursue his other passions, including fly fishing, mountain climbing, and exploring the waters of the West in his canoe.

To learn more about John's seminars, audio tapes, and other resources for the heart, visit his Web site at: www.ransomed heart.com or write to: